Eden and the Individual: Christianity for the 21st Century

Emil Mihelich

Dr. Skinner,

I appreciate your paraphrase of Descartes: "I am, therefore I think." I hope this book lives up to that responsibility.

Sincerely,
Emil Mihelich

iUniverse, Inc.
New York Lincoln Shanghai

Eden and the Individual: Christianity for the 21st Century

Copyright © 2006 by Emil Mihelich

All rights reserved. No part of this book may be used or reproduced by any means, graphic, electronic, or mechanical, including photocopying, recording, taping or by any information storage retrieval system without the written permission of the publisher except in the case of brief quotations embodied in critical articles and reviews.

iUniverse books may be ordered through booksellers or by contacting:

iUniverse
2021 Pine Lake Road, Suite 100
Lincoln, NE 68512
www.iuniverse.com
1-800-Authors (1-800-288-4677)

ISBN-13: 978-0-595-40214-4 (pbk)
ISBN-13: 978-0-595-84590-3 (ebk)
ISBN-10: 0-595-40214-3 (pbk)
ISBN-10: 0-595-84590-8 (ebk)

Printed in the United States of America

Eden and the Individual: Christianity for the 21st Century

To individuals everywhere who provide the focus
for our wondrous mythic imagination.

"It is not Christianity, but our conception of it, that has become antiquated in the face of the present world situation."

—Dr. C. G. Jung,
"The Undiscovered Self," 1958

Contents

Foreword		xi
Introduction		xv
CHAPTER 1	Christianity and the Universal World of Story	1
CHAPTER 2	After the Moonwalk: The End of our Mythological Age	13
CHAPTER 3	Existentialism: The Godless Philosophy of God	27
CHAPTER 4	The Heart of Rock n' Roll	39
CHAPTER 5	The Undiscovered Morality of Amor	52
CHAPTER 6	From the Cathedral to the Shopping Mall	64
CHAPTER 7	Baseball: America's Universal Game	75
CHAPTER 8	Indian Yoga and the Psychology of Western Creative Mythology	84
CHAPTER 9	An Answer to Carl Jung's "Answer to Job"	97
CHAPTER 10	The Nuclear Age: A Time for Heroes	109
CHAPTER 11	Mythological Illiteracy: The Western World's Folly	121
CHAPTER 12	At the Crossroads: The Crucifix or the Golden Arch	132
CHAPTER 13	In Search of Morality	141

CHAPTER 14	A Matter of Time..........................	152
About the Author	....	163

Foreword

I'm sure I can trace my interest in the Garden of Eden story back to my dad's death in July of 1950. He died at the age of 41, just six days before my sixth birthday. I didn't know much about the nature of time and death when I was six, but I did know about the Garden of Eden, God, Adam and Eve and original sin. I was old enough to know that, according to the accepted interpretation of the Eden story, Adam and Eve's sin introduced death into the world. My dad had died which, according to the standard interpretation of the creation story once again, made Adam and Eve responsible for his death. If they would have avoided sin in the Garden, I would have had my dad forever.

Of course, my world was very small when I was six. It didn't include someone else's dad, for example, who might have died under similar circumstances. Thus the Church's interpretation of the Eden story made sense—until I started to think about it. The more I thought, the more I realized I couldn't dislike Adam and Eve in spite of their sin. In fact, I actually found myself taking a liking to Eve. Where Adam was somewhat reticent, she seemed to have some spunk. She reminded me, I think, of my own grandmother and my own mother, neither of whom ever would be accused of reticence. If Eve reminded me of them, how could I see her as some selfish, gullible woman who didn't care about jeopardizing anyone's paradise? I received my first communion when I was seven, but it didn't take me long to question the Church's understanding of the Garden of Eden story. And I couldn't help thinking that I probably would have eaten the apple myself—had I been given the chance.

But my thoughts about Adam, Eve, Eden, death and God remained private. I learned my catechism with the proper respect and devotion, without ever asking the question I kept contemplating privately. I never publicly asked if my dad would have lived had Adam and Eve not disobeyed God and listened to the serpent. To hold back on such a question may seem ludicrous, and even unbelievable, these days. However, in the days before the Roman Catholic Church's Second Vatican Council—the 1962–65 ecumenical gathering of church leaders called, in part, to meet the apparent scientific threat to established religion—believers thought more than twice about questioning that church's authoritative teaching. We all knew about Hell, but more importantly we all knew about the nature of Adam and Eve's original sin. None of us were eager to disobey and repeat that sin. None of us wanted to live a life of pride.

Still, when I was a sophomore in high school, my curiosity got the best of me. I finally asked—out loud and within full earshot of all my classmates—if my dad would have died had Adam and Eve decided to obey God and leave the apple alone. My religion teacher was an Irish Christian Brother and an honorable man of duty who had no intention of lying to me. But when he said yes, your dad would have lived if Adam and Eve hadn't decided to eat the apple, I was no longer six years old. In all honesty I couldn't believe his answer, and with that epiphany I think this work was born. From that moment on death became natural for me, and thus life itself became just as naturally monstrous.

What follows on the succeeding pages are my thoughts and conclusions on a series of topics that, taken together as a cohesive whole, represent my attempt to define the role of the responsible individual at the dawning of a new epoch that has witnessed the waning of the power and influence of institutional authority. The Garden of Eden story, supported by its traditional, historic reading, provided the foundation for that influence, but times have changed. If the historic reading of the Eden story is irrelevant in the Age of Rational Science, the story itself is not. I've wondered about that story, and the mythology built on it, since my childhood encounter with the reality of death, and I'm convinced that the serpent deserves a better fate. At the same time, I'm just as convinced that, contrary to traditional thought, Adam and Eve avoided sin by eating the apple. They did disobey authority, but in so doing they obeyed a more benevolent authority and thus provided clear direction for the course of a responsible, individual life in a world where death is natural.

I don't consider myself a follower of Carl Jung, Joseph Campbell or Loren Eiseley, but I do admit to a powerful connection to all three—especially to Dr. Jung and Mr. Campbell. I offer no apologies for the attachment. I found allies for my own, independent thought in their work, and by building on their conclusions, maybe I can begin where they left off. I'm not interested in being controversial or inflammatory, but I am interested in exploring life's infinite possibilities. Without the haunting specter of original sin, I think we're free to explore those possibilities, always celebrated in the mythological realm where time knows no specific duration. I don't mean to persuade, but I do mean to argue. I hope my arguments, built on Eden's 'Serpent Premise,' can be as cogent for the dawning Age of the Individual as the traditional arguments, built on Eden's 'Yahwistic Premise,' were for the waning Age of the Institution. The transition has been far from smooth, but as Nick Carraway reminds us in 'The Great

Gatsby,' F. Scott Fitzgerald's tale of 1920s' "Jazz-age" excess: "So we beat on, boats against the current, borne back ceaselessly into the past."

And by revisiting what was, we can discover what could be.

Emil Mihelich
Spring, 2006

Introduction

Any attempt to redefine Christianity for the 21st century and beyond has to begin by paying homage to St. Augustine, the father of Christian orthodoxy. Augustine's formative idea of the City of God, that supplied institutional Christianity with both its structural form and doctrinal substance, still is—and always will be—a necessary idea. But his conclusions built on that idea, as well as the resulting psychological, philosophical and ethical way of life that followed, can become obsolete when examined in the light of contemporary scientific discovery. However, Augustinian sacrifice and commitment to belief that led to those conclusions, presented—argumentatively—in his monumental work aptly entitled 'The City of God,' never can become obsolete. By revisiting institutional Christianity, with equal sacrifice and commitment, we can redefine St. Augustine's idea of the City of God to give it—and Christianity itself—continuing life in the 21st century and the centuries to follow.

Any revisiting of Augustinian Christianity has to start with the Garden of Eden story because any understanding of the Christian mythological heritage depends on the believer's interpretation of that creation myth. St. Augustine's City of God is a Yahwistic City built on the premise that accepts "God" in Eden as being the authentic, One True God superior to all other "gods." In contrast, the 21st century City of God is a Serpent City built on the premise that accepts the Serpent as the authentic God of the formative Eden story. The Serpent, then, resides in the individual, in the "psyche," and can be brought to life while that individual lives. Thus the Serpent City of God is an earthly city to whose creation all individuals can contribute. St. Augustine's institutionally defining work, 'The City of God,' offers a clear, coherent and cogent expression of mythological promise—as governed by his concept of time and by his scientific understanding of the world around him. The 21st century's answer to Augustine's rhetorical majesty can offer a similarly clear, coherent and cogent expression of that promise—as governed by our concept of time and by our scientific understanding of the world around us.

Dr. Carl Jung, in his distinguished work 'The Undiscovered Self,' commented that he was "convinced that it is not Christianity, but our conception of it, that has become antiquated in the face of the present world situation." Our "conception" of Christianity has been shaped by Augustinian conclusions logically presented in 'The City of God.' Our "antiquated" "conception" of Christianity can give way to a more applicable, contemporary "conception" if we view what Dr. Jung called "the Christian symbol" as, he continues, "a living thing that carries within itself the seeds of further development."

Christianity, as revealed in the Old and New Testament, offered St. Augustine the certainty he was searching for in contrast to the more speculative thought associated with traditional philosophy from Plato to Porphyry. The sacred scriptures offered what Augustine saw as Divine Wisdom that had to be superior to any mere human wisdom. With that biblical authority providing him with necessary support, St. Augustine was able to create a solid, logical argument built on the premise that accepted Yahweh—the 'God' in Eden—as The One True God and Creator of the Universe.

The Yahwistic logic that followed, and that governed the moral and ethical conduct of the individuals subject to its influence, carried with it the weight of truth as long as its major premise could be accepted as being true itself. St. Augustine's thought, embraced by the established, imperially supported Orthodox Church of the fifth century, emerged as a philosophy of the masses. That philosophy, that mythological structure, outlined a noble purpose to life that, in turn, offered the obedient individual the reward of eternal citizenship in the Heavenly City of God. The disobedient individual faced the alternative to this reward—an eternity of punishment in the equally majestic, subterranean Kingdom of Hell. Fear of that "Dark" Kingdom helped create an aura of obedience to a mythological structure which then provided for the moral, psychological and philosophical certainty that characterized Augustine's argument—built on the acceptance of Adam and Eve's original sin in the Garden of Eden.

To this day Augustine's thought remains—and will remain—a powerful testament to logical validity. But the conception of time that governed his thought and the scientific understanding that accompanied it no longer can apply to any equally committed and equally sacrificial thought that may characterize our day. Augustine's Yahwistic, original sin "Grand Design" remains logically valid, but examined in light of contemporary scientific exploration and discovery, it no longer carries with it the weight of truth. Augustine's Yahwistic, original sin premise is not true when we view it in relation to our contemporary concept of time and the accompanying scientific understanding of the universe. Thus it is time to revisit Augustinian Christianity, in accord with contemporary science, to recapture the mythological structure that can provide for necessary moral, psychological and philosophical certainty.

Without revisiting Augustinian Christianity, whether individually or collectively, we are left with moral, psychological and philosophical uncertainty where, at best, everything is "relative." And the mythological order that accompanied the once-established certainty is reduced to chaos, which is the natural result of the inevitable disintegration of Augustine's "Grand Design" built on his Yahwistic, original sin foundation. That major premise carries with it the weight of truth only if the incidents described in the Eden story are historically and scientifically accurate, in the manner St. Augustine accepted them. To accept them as such in his era—and probably even as late as July of 1969, when America's Apollo astronauts, Neil Armstrong and Buzz Aldrin, landed on the moon—is understandable and even convincing. But that same acceptance, given our contemporary, scientific understanding of time and the universe, is neither understandable nor convincing today when we have stepped across the threshold of the 21st century.

To retreat into that acceptance in the face of visible moral, psychological and philosophical chaos is to retreat into a past that cannot, and should not, be recaptured. Such a retreat into obsolescence, no matter how impressive the numbers, is more destructive than creative. It is to turn that which once was true into a lie because we cannot "live the afternoon of life according to the program of life's morning," as Dr. Jung concludes in his study of the 'Stages of Life.' To revisit Augustinian Christianity, to discover the Serpent as the authentic God of Eden and to reason from that premise—free from the constraints of original sin—is to follow the more creative path in the face of the life-threatening chaos that characterizes our day. By following that path we can discover the moral, psychological and philosophical certainty that is compatible with our contemporary understanding of time and its accompanying, scientific explanation of the creation of the human race and of the universe itself.

The 21st-century answer to fifth-century Augustinian Christianity, now reflective of the majesty that was, should present a clear and cogent vision of the majesty that could be. In that regard the 21st-century answer should represent the fulfillment of Dante's statement of faith that he expressed to St. Peter at the gates of Paradise in his 'Divine Comedy.' When St. Peter asked him about the meaning of faith, Dante replied: "Faith is the substance of the things we hope for and an argument for the things unseen." Examined in that light, Augustinian Christianity is a statement of faith commensurate with the scientific knowledge of his time—held together, until the mid-20th century, by the imposing force of the Church. The 21st-century answer to Augustine's fifth-century orthodoxy should offer a similar statement of faith—only it has to be commensurate with the wondrous scientific knowledge of our day that only can become more wondrous in the days to come. As a statement of faith, Christianity for the 21st century has to be reinforced, rather than refuted, by that scientific knowledge.

Christianity for the 21st century, in redefining Augustine's idea of institutional supremacy, can only present a clear vision of the fulfillment that could be. It cannot present a clear vision of the fulfillment that will be. Christianity for the 21st century and beyond leaves it up to the individual, inspired by love and not motivated by fear, to live as an incarnate expression of its creative vision. It is a vision of faith built on the Serpent premise, and the volumes of "creative mythology" representing the literary heritage of Western civilization, from Homeric Greece to Faulknerian America, constitute its sacred scripture. The moral, psychological and philosophical certainty presented in Christianity for the 21st century is that expressed repeatedly in "the Hero with a thousand faces"—with the "face" of Christ being one of those "thousand." And that body of "creative mythology," in contrast to the "traditional mythology" of the orthodox authority, provides Christianity for the 21st century with the authority it needs to match that of its Augustinian counterpart born in the fifth century.

The Augustinian epoch of the Christian era of Western civilization is over. To revisit Augustinian Christianity is to meet the challenge that ending presents. As mythologist Joseph Campbell declares in 'The Hero with a Thousand Faces': "Only birth can defeat death." Revisiting the Garden of Eden story, and the original sin mythology built upon it, can lead to that birth. It can lead to the birth of a contemporary "Serpent Christianity"—as opposed to the "antiquated" "Yahwistic Christianity"—that, consciously realized, can offer the 21st century and beyond a clear, coherent and cogent vision of the mythological promise that awaits us all.

1

Christianity and the Universal World of Story

Throughout the Christian era of Western civilization, we have built our faith in Christianity on its accepted historical reading. Thus we have seen it as being a record of something done and therefore believable and true, existing apart from, rather than a part of, the made-up—and ultimately unbelievable and false—world of story. However, with the close of the 20th century individual experience and the discoveries of rational science—at the very least—combine to question Christianity's status as being primarily a record of something done and—at the very most—combine to threaten its existence as a viable, affective force in the life of the Christian West as we emerge into the 21st century and beyond. In the interests of preserving our religion, and thus the very structure and foundation of our civilization, the conditions of our era dictate that we seriously read Christianity as being something made up and therefore as being a part of, as opposed to being apart from, the more universal world of story.

Our world consists of stories primarily designed to entertain and those primarily designed to inspire with the latter contributions occupying the more exalted ground—the ground of mythology. The history of Christianity in Western civilization proves that it deserves to occupy a portion of this exalted ground. Christianity carries the inspirational power of a world mythology whose majesty has given birth to individual, local mythologies that, when taken collectively, constitute the great literature of our civilization's Christian era. Christianity belongs in this made-up, universal world of story. Both individually accumulated experience and the discoveries of rational science demand that we see it as such to tap its power and provide life, collectively and individually, with a noble purpose now and in the decades and centuries to follow.

Dr. Carl Jung, in his autobiography entitled 'Memories, Dreams, and Reflections,' comments that mythology "expresses life more precisely than does science." Mythologist Joseph Campbell elaborates on this idea and distinguishes between two types of mythology in 'Creative Mythology,' the fourth and final volume of his study of the 'Masks of God':

> In the context of a traditional mythology the symbols are presented in socially maintained rites, through which the individual is required to experience, or will pretend to have experienced, certain insights, sentiments, and commitments. In what I am calling creative mythology, on the other hand, this order is reversed: the individual has had an experience of his own—of order, horror, beauty, or mere exhilaration—which he seeks to communicate through signs; and if his realization has been of a certain depth and import, his communication will have the value and force of living myth—for those, that is to say, who receive and respond to it themselves, with recognition, uncoerced.

Christianity, when we read it primarily as a record of something done, is not a creative mythology. Rather, it is a "traditional" or "collective" mythology of authority more "coercive" than "evocative," as Mr. Campbell would say. It imposes a structure on life and gives it meaning and direction only as long as no outside force, such as individual experience or the discoveries of rational science, threatens the historicity of its facts. When either, or any, such force threatens that historicity, however, the imposed structure crumbles. Life, both individually and collectively, then loses meaning and direction as reflected in the psychological chaos that characterizes the post-World War II world of Western civilization. But when we read Christianity as an expression of something made up in the manner of story, it emerges as a "creative mythology of a certain depth and import" that can have "the value and force of living myth—for those, that is to say, who receive and respond to it themselves, with recognition, uncoerced."

When life loses its meaning and direction, either individually or collectively, it loses its sense of adventure as well as individuals lose sight of "certain insights, sentiments, and commitments" supposed to be experienced as a result of exposure to "traditional" mythology and its "socially maintained rites." Christianity, recognized as such a "traditional" mythology, had the "value and force of living myth"—the "value" and "force" to provide life with a sense of adventure—as long as neither accumulated experience nor the discoveries of rational science threatened its claims to truth, established—primarily—on its status of being a historical record of something done. In light of the current challenge to that historicity, presented by both accumulated experience and scientific discovery, only a "creative" mythology can have "the value and force of living myth" to restore to life its meaning and direction as well as its sense of adventure. When we read it primarily as an expression of something made up, Christianity "springs not, like theology," as Mr. Campbell continues in the same final volume of his study of the 'Masks of God,' "from the dicta of authority, but from the insights, sentiments, thought, and vision of an adequate individual, loyal to his own experience of value." As a result, a "creative" mythology "corrects authority holding to the shells of forms produced and left behind by lives once lived." In the process of correcting authority, a "creative" mythology renews "the act of experience itself," and, in addition, "restores to existence the quality of adventure"—the adventure that is lost when the imposed structure of the "traditional" mythology crumbles in the face of the challenge of accumulated individual experience and the discoveries of rational science.

"Creative" mythology, then, is born out of experience. It is made up, but it is made up from that experience and thus lives as an expression of its truth. The commitment and conviction of the artist, the "adequate individual loyal to his own experience of value," gives the work "the value and force of living myth" which, in turn, gives individual men and women the chance to respond to it "with recognition, uncoerced." However, before we can respond, we have to acknowledge such a "creative" mythology as being believable, as being a source of truth—the truth of experience. And we have to read it primarily as an expression of something made up to recognize its "value" and to feel its "force." Therefore, before we can respond to Christianity, we have to see it as a "creative" mythology that "corrects authority holding to the shells of forms produced and left behind by lives once lived."

When we read it as a "traditional" mythology, Christianity is more closely related to theology because it then springs "from the dicta of authority" rather than from the "insights, sentiments, thought, and vision of an adequate individual, loyal to his own experience of value." Thus when we view Christianity as a "traditional" mythology, we see it as being separate from, and even superior to, the made up world of story which includes the exalted ground occupied by "creative" mythology. But when we read it as a "creative" mythology, with its crucifixion event taken as its fundamental, structuring image, Christianity is neither separate from nor superior to the world of story and its exalted ground. Instead, we see it reflected repeatedly in that same made-up world through Joseph Campbell's "Hero with a thousand faces." And to the American audience perhaps the most familiar, even if still undiscovered, "face" of this universal hero is that of Huckleberry Finn found in Mark Twain's premier contribution to the exalted ground of "creative" mythology—'The Adventures of Huckleberry Finn.'

Twain, undeniably, made up his American classic. Understandably, then, we don't hesitate to question its status as a "creative" mythology equivalent in "depth and import," as well as in "value" and "force," to Christianity. However, when we read it through the eyes of an "adequate individual"—acknowledging Huck's decision to go to Hell and to tear up his note revealing the hiding place of Jim, Miss Watson's runaway slave and Huck's companion in adventure, as its fundamental, structuring image—'The Adventures of Huckleberry Finn' "springs not, like theology, from the dicta of authority, but from insights, sentiments, thoughts, and vision of a adequate individual, loyal to his own experience of value." Huck could have sent his note to Miss Watson in obedience to both the prevailing social authority and the reinforcing pulpit, ecclesiastical authority. But rather than choosing to betray Jim and his trust, he chose, instead, to obey "his own experience of value," even if his act of having to disobey to obey meant he would have to spend eternity amidst the fires of Hell that had to be as real for him—and for any authentic, 19th century believer—as were the waters of the Mississippi River. And when those same curious eyes of the "adequate individual," made curious by the demands of our day, examine Christianity as being something made up and when they focus on its crucifixion event, we can see that these structuring images—the tearing up of the note and the crucifixion, as well as the stories they support—are born out of the individual's common experience with "the authority holding to the shells of forms produced and left behind by lives once lived."

In the story of Christ, supported by the structuring image of the crucifixion, the Pharisaic authority of the Old Testament holds "to the shells of forms produced and left behind by lives once lived." In the story of Huckleberry Finn, supported by the structuring image of Huck tearing up his note, the Christian church and its pulpit-centered Christianity plays that same role. Thus when we read it primarily as an expression of something made up and necessarily part of the world of story, the story of Christ—Christianity with the crucifixion event taken as its fundamental, structuring image—essentially becomes—like the story of Huckleberry Finn almost 1900 years later—an expression of the conflict that develops between "an adequate individual" and an Old Testament authority "holding to the shells of forms produced and left behind by lives once lived." And when, with curious eyes, we view the exalted ground of the world of story as being made up from experience, we can see "the act of experience itself" renewed and we can see the restoration "to existence the quality of adventure." We can see the truth of experience by which an individual can live to participate in that adventure.

In his essay entitled 'The Stages of Life' Dr. Carl Jung states:

> We cannot live the afternoon of life according to the program of life's morning; for what was great in the morning will be little at evening, and what in the morning was true will in the evening have become a lie.

To curious eyes, accepting the exalted ground of the world of story as being believable, as being a made-up source of truth—the truth of experience—both the story of Christ and the story of Huckleberry Finn reflect the pattern Dr. Jung identifies. Both Christ and Huck qualify as "adequate individuals, loyal to their own experience of value" who find themselves in conflict with an authority that their experience tells them, either consciously or unconsciously, is archaic and in need of correction. The "program of life's morning" to which Dr. Jung refers would be, in the story of Christ, that reflected in the Pharisaic authority. In the story of Huckleberry Finn the "program" would be that reflected in the Christian church and its pulpit-centered Christianity. The Pharisaic authority and the Christian church authority represent Old Testament authority in their respective stories while the "insights, sentiments, thoughts, and vision of an adequate individual, loyal to his own experience of value" represent New Testament responses to Old Testament obsolescence. These New Testament responses, then, whether we find them in the story of Christ or the story of Huckleberry Finn, are "creative" responses to "traditional" authority. By the "afternoon of life" such authority only holds to "shells of forms produced" with its substance no longer generating the "value and force of living myth" for anyone who still may be open to responding to it "of themselves, with recognition, uncoerced."

Only "creative" responses generate the "value and force of living myth." Only the "creative" mythology of Christ and Huckleberry Finn generates the specific "value" and "force" to renew "the act of experience itself" and restore "to existence the quality of adventure." Thus the "creative" mythology of Christ and Huckleberry Finn represents the substance of the program for the "afternoon of life" where the "traditional" mythology of the Pharisaic and Christian authority has come into conflict with the inspiration of an "adequate" individual's experience. And the "adequate individual"—the heroic individual—resolves the conflict by obeying "his own experience of value" and not the "dicta of authority." Consciously or unconsciously, such an individual illuminates the path that "corrects authority holding to the shells of forms produced" whose substance, once "great" and "true in the morning," has become "little" and "a lie in the evening."

When we read it primarily as an expression of something made up, the story of Christ—centered around the crucifixion—is reflected in the universal world of story represented by the story of Huckleberry Finn—centered around Huck's tearing up of his note. If the story of Huckleberry Finn deserves to occupy a portion of the exalted ground of "creative" mythology, so does the story of Christ. Thus the two stories are equivalent expressions of the same idea. Constituting a "creative" mythology having the potential of "renewing the act of experience itself" and of restoring "to existence the quality of adventure," both stories come into conflict with the orthodox, or "traditional," mythology of the Pharisaic and Christian authorities—both of which are built on the premise that acknowledges an individual's nature as being essentially sinful.

Such a premise, requiring the human race to atone for its corrupt nature, has "the value and force of living myth" as long as it, and its accompanying mythology, doesn't conflict with any force lying beyond its orthodox boundaries. If the idea of the individual being essentially sinful were natural to the human species, the succeeding accumulation of experience would reinforce that orthodox, "traditional" idea—identifying it with Joseph Campbell's "elementary idea" or with Jung's "archetypal idea." Then we would grow into the accompanying mythology as a result of our experience in the world outside the traditional orthodoxy. However, the stories of Christ and Huckleberry Finn show that for the "adequate individual"—the obedient, heroic individual—the natural accumulation of experience produces the opposite effect. It refutes, rather than reinforces, the established orthodox idea and, at the same time, destroys "the value and force" that the accompanying "traditional" mythology once had as "living myth." With the "traditional" mythology discredited and with its "socially maintained rites" subsequently rendered powerless, "adequate" individuals are left with their "creative" mythology whose experiential, "evocative" premise—in contrast to its orthodox, "coercive" counterpart—expresses an idea that warrants being accorded the status of "elementary" or "archetypal."

The made-up world of story, reflecting the concrete world of experience, provides ample evidence of humankind's capacity for sin. It provides numerous examples of individuals living in response to their will to pleasure or their will to power that we see expressed in the structure of both the Pharisaic authority in the story of Christ and the Christian authority in the story of Huckleberry Finn. A close, curious study of the "adequate individual"—the heroic individual—reveals, however, another dimension of the complex nature of the individual human being. It reveals a dimension that carries "creative" mythology beyond the boundaries of the "traditional" mythology of the Pharisaic and Christian authorities. While acknowledging our capacity to recognize and live in response to our will to pleasure or power, the "creative" mythology of Christ and Huckleberry Finn identifies and celebrates our additional capacity to recognize and live in response to—in obedience to—our will to love. Whereas the "traditional" mythology of the Pharisaic and Christian authority, in its program for "life's morning," promotes the idea that the individual essentially is sin, the "creative" mythology of Christ and Huckleberry Finn, in its program for life's "afternoon," promotes the idea that the individual essentially is love. The "adequate individual"—the heroic individual—expressed through the "faces" of Christ and Huckleberry Finn, arrives at this conviction not through submission to the "dicta of authority" but through obedience to "his own experience of value." The natural accumulation of experience leads the "adequate individual"—the heroic individual—to recognize the "elementary" and "archetypal" idea identifying love as representing the essence of any human being. And that individual lives, either consciously or unconsciously, in correction of "the authority holding to the shells of forms produced and left behind by lives once lived."

When we read it primarily as a record of historical facts, the story of Christ, in opposition to the story of Huckleberry Finn, directs the individual—whose nature essentially is sin—along the path of atonement with God—separate from His creations—through obedience to His laws expressed through the "traditional" mythology of the Pharisaic and Christian authority. This program of atonement, "presented in socially maintained rites," has the "value and force of living myth" as long as its main premise does not come into conflict with naturally accumulated experience or with the discoveries of rational science. Thus this "traditional" program of atonement, whether Pharisaic or Christian, has the power to direct its collective individuals toward a noble purpose of life only in the morning of that life. This same program, with its "traditional" mythology "presented in socially maintained rites" discredited either by naturally accumulated experience or by the discoveries of rational science, has no power to provide its collective individuals with such direction in the "afternoon of life."

However, when we read it primarily in the manner of story, as an expression of experiential facts, the story of Christ, centered around his crucifixion and in accord with the story of Huckleberry Finn—centered around Huck's tearing up of his note—directs the individual, whose nature essentially is love, along a path of at-one-ment with God, as one with humankind, through obedience to His laws revealed through the natural accumulation of experience. This program of at-one-ment, the "adequate" individual's—the heroic individual's—"realization" of "a certain depth and import," carries "the value and force of living myth" forever. Its main premise does not come into conflict with naturally accumulated experience nor, as is the case with the Christian authority's continuing claims to historicity, with the discoveries of rational science—particularly Jung's psychological discoveries. Thus this program of at-one-ment, this "creative" mythology, whether expressed in the story of Christ or in the story of Huckleberry Finn, always had—and will continue to have—the power to direct "adequate" individuals—heroic individuals—toward a noble purpose of life. Furthermore, this same program, with its "creative" mythology expressed through corrected authority and supported by "socially maintained rites," could, in the "afternoon of life," afford its collective individuals the opportunity to "experience"—or at least to "pretend to have experienced"—certain "insights, sentiments, and commitments" always lived by alienated, but "adequate," heroic individuals "loyal to their own experience of value."

When we see them with eyes made curious by accumulated experience and the discoveries of rational science, the stories of Christ and Huckleberry Finn become expressions of New Testament, "creative" mythology that presents a program of at-one-ment in opposition to the Old Testament, "traditional" mythology of the Pharisaic and Christian authority that presents a program of atonement. The New Testament, "creative" mythology is a mythology of love reinforced by naturally accumulated experience and, in accord with Jung's psychological conclusions, the discoveries of rational science. If we read Christianity a part of the world of story, we read it rationally and sensibly. In the process we help preserve the foundation and structure of Western civilization. And when we read it rationally and sensibly, we discover the "elementary" and "archetypal" idea of love—previously undiscovered but now made Flesh in the "adequate," heroic individual who, regardless of his or her "face," remains "loyal to his own experience of value" and "corrects authority holding to the shells of forms produced and left behind by lives once lived."

As 'The Adventures of Huckleberry Finn' reveals, the Old Testament mythology of sin still was in effect by the late 19th century, preserved by the Christian church that Huck had to disobey in order to live his will to love. Like Adam and Eve, in the Old Testament Garden of Eden story, he faced a conflict of obedience. And he chose, as did Adam and Eve, to obey the Laws of Experience, the Way of the Cross illuminated by a rational reading of the story of Christ that is centered around his crucifixion. When we read it is as part of, rather than apart from, the more universal world of story, the Old Testament Eden story and the New Testament Christ story not only reinforce each other but also they are reinforced by the 19th century Huckleberry Finn story. The three stories, then, become different expressions of a unified, "creative" mythology that, as the program for "the afternoon of life," carries the "value and force of living myth—for those, that is to say, who receive and respond to it themselves with recognition uncoerced."

This program for "the afternoon of life" is not necessarily different or new. More accurately, it represents a fresh understanding of an established program that served life's morning. It is a fresh understanding consistent with both the facts revealed by naturally accumulated experience and those discovered through rational, scientific inquiry. The Garden of Eden story supplied the foundation for the program of "life's morning," and it remains the foundation of the program for "the afternoon of life." The understanding of Christianity as a "traditional" mythology based on it being apart from, and even superior to, the more universal world of story is archaic. But Christianity itself, as a "creative" mythology based upon it being a part of, and reflected in, that more universal world, remains vitally alive. It carries the power to free collective individuals and to guide them to the discovery of their potential, and their responsibility, to live as "adequate," heroic individuals, regardless of their "face"—male or female without distinction or discrimination.

Human beings are not "condemned to be free," as Jean-Paul Sartre says. On the contrary, individuals are destined to be free as expressed in New Testament "creative" mythology. Furthermore, a True, Authentic, Loving God would seek to awaken that destiny within His children. He would want His children to be free. He would seek to illuminate the path of enlightenment to give them the opportunity to be free. He would not seek to prevent that natural enlightenment to keep His children in obedience to Him out of response to His own will to pleasure or to power. The authentic God must live His will to love if He expects His children to believe in that same will.

Thus in the New Testament, "creative" mythology, the "God" of the Garden of Eden story cannot be the True, Authentic God that the Old Testament, "traditional" mythology claims Him to be. In the New Testament, "creative" mythology the Authentic, Universal God—who out of love seeks to illuminate for His children the path of freedom—is the serpent. Moreover, the Serpent of Eden, in seeking to set His children free, prefigures Christ who—out of love and because of his courage to live that will—endures the agony of the crucifixion to illuminate that same path of freedom—the Way of the Cross that the children of God have to walk to reach their destiny. Both the serpent and Christ are expressions of the God of Experience in opposition to the God of Authority. And if God is Love, this God of Experience, who resides within and who is awakened in the "adequate," heroic individual by the natural accumulation of experience, is the Authentic, Universal God. The God of Experience reflects the heroic essence of individual human beings, male and female without distinction or discrimination—the "undiscovered self" in reference to the scientific, psychological thought of Carl Jung.

By obeying the God of Experience—the serpent power—in opposition to the God of Authority, Huckleberry Finn lives that "undiscovered self" previously expressed in all its majesty in Adam and Eve and in the agonized Christ nailed to his Cross of Freedom. Huck lives his will to love even if it means spending eternity in the Christian authority's Hell. But the Hell of the Old Testament, "traditional" mythology is not the Hell of the New Testament, "creative" mythology. If Huck would have chosen to obey authority in disobedience to his naturally awakened responsibility, he would have chosen to live in Hell whose psychic agony is a match for any physical agony associated with the Hell of the Old Testament, "traditional" mythology. Neither Adam and Eve, nor Christ nor Huckleberry Finn chose alienation. They chose freedom that results in alienation only because the Old Testament authority, whether Pharisaic or Christian and holding to its "traditional" mythology, insists that God is separate from His creations. The alienation of the individual, revealed as an "adequate" or heroic individual in the New Testament, "creative" mythology, decreases in direct proportion to the number of individuals who—when given the chance—choose to obey their awakened responsibility and live their destiny "themselves, with recognition, uncoerced."

This New Testament, "creative" mythology is one of awakened responsibility and love whereas the Old Testament, "traditional" mythology is one of imposed rules and sin. Both the New Testament, "creative" mythology for the "afternoon of life" and the Old Testament, "traditional" mythology of "life's morning" present programs that emphasize the value of obedience to the Laws of God as a life-directing force. And both mythologies emphasize punishment and agony that results from disobeying those Laws. However, according to the program for the "afternoon of life" expressed in the New Testament "creative" mythology, the punishment for disobeying the Laws of God, revealed through naturally accumulated experience, has to be self-imposed because New Testament, "creative" mythology does not separate God from the individual. Therefore, in accord with the evidence of experience and the discoveries of rational science, the agony associated with such punishment has to be measured in terms of psychic agony to be experienced here and now as the individual lives in the concrete world of experience. We cannot measure the agony in terms of physical agony, imposed from without, to be experienced later in another world created by the offended God, separate from individual human beings, to house His disobedient servants.

Joseph Campbell, in 'Creative Mythology,' refers to this Old Testament premise of the separation of God and the individual, whether expressed through the Pharisaic or Christian authority, as "mythic dissociation." And he continues by indicating that the individual can achieve a relationship with this separate God only through participation "in a specific social group." In the case of the Pharisaic, Old Testament, "traditional" mythology built on the Eden foundation, this "specific social group" is the "Holy Race" with whom "that God had concluded a covenant." In the case of the Christian, Old Testament, "traditional" mythology built on that same foundation, this "specific social group" is "Christ's Church." Thus the individual either has to be born into the "Holy Race" or initiated through baptism ("spiritual birth") "into membership in Christ's Church" to achieve this relationship with God that Mr. Campbell calls "social identification."

That "social identification" presented through "socially maintained rites," functions as "living myth" as long as its main premise of "mythic dissociation" is not discredited either by the natural accumulation of experience or by the discoveries of rational science. In his thorough study of the 'Masks of God,' that concludes with 'Creative Mythology,' Mr. Campbell describes the contemporary status of Christianity as a "traditional" mythology built on the premise of "mythic dissociation" and the subsequent "social identification":

> Unhappily, however, in the light of what is now known, not only of the history of the Bible and the Church, but also of the universe and the evolution of the species, a suspicion has been confirmed that was already dawning in the Middle Ages; namely that the biblical myth of Creation, Fall, and Redemption is historically untrue. Hence, there now has spread throughout the Christian world a desolating sense of not only of no divinity within (mythic dissociation), but also, of no participation in divinity without (social identification dissolved): and that, in short, is the mythological base of the Waste Land of the modern soul, or, as it is being called these days, our "alienation."

However, the alienation resulting from "mythic dissociation" and "social identification dissolved" is not that identified in the "adequate individual"—the heroic individual—found in "creative" mythology. The alienation of the "adequate," heroic individual results from his or her decision to obey the Laws of God as revealed through naturally accumulated experience—those Laws and that God never acknowledged as authentic by orthodox authority, whether Pharisaic or Christian.

When we look with curious eyes, made so by thousands of years of experience, and in turn supported by the discoveries of rational science, we can see that we live in an era where our cherished "traditional" mythology—built on the premise of "mythic dissociation" and the subsequent "social identification" supported by "socially maintained rites"—has lost its "value and force as living myth." And that loss results in what Mr. Campbell identifies as "the Waste Land of the modern soul." Fortunately, however, those same, curious eyes can lead us beyond the recognition of the obsolescence of our "traditional" program of atonement. They can lead us to the recognition of our "creative" program of at-one-ment that we previously had no conscious need to discover. Luckily, we continually expressed that program in our world of story—that universal, exalted ground that celebrates our capacity to live as "adequate individuals," as heroic individuals, in obedience to the Laws of God revealed through naturally accumulated experience.

The Western world's Christianity, accepted as part of the universal world of story and its exalted ground, is such a "creative" program of at-one-ment. It is a "creative" mythology that corrects authority "holding to the shells of forms produced and left behind by lives once lived." Referring to "creative" mythology, Campbell continues in his final volume of the 'Masks of God':

> Renewing the act of experience itself, it restores to existence the quality of adventure, at once shattering and reintegrating the fixed, already known, in the sacrificial, creative fire of the becoming thing that is no such thing at all but life, not as it <u>will be</u> or as it <u>should be</u>, as it <u>was</u> or as <u>it never will be</u>, but as it <u>is</u>, in depth, in process, <u>here and now</u>, inside and out.

When we read it with curious eyes, as part of the more universal world of story, Christianity stands tall among that world's exalted monuments to the individual's capacity to create. As with any "creative" mythology, it is alive with the "sacrificial, creative fire of the becoming thing that is no thing at all but life…as it is, in depth, <u>in process</u>, <u>here and now</u>, inside and out." Christianity's Adam and Eve, its Christ and its Huckleberry Finn represent only four "faces" of the "adequate individual"—the "Hero with a thousand faces"—who challenges us to answer the at-one-ment call of the serpent and to live our destiny to heal "the Waste Land" of the individual and collective "modern soul."

2

After the Moonwalk: The End of our Mythological Age

The human race's historical emergence, though undeniably accompanied by various acts of violence, deception and treachery, nonetheless is most accurately characterized by a continuing quest to understand—a quest fueled, individually and collectively, by a sense of awe and wonder at the world and its promise of adventure. Thus we have numerous examples of the solitary quest of the artist each in his or her own way being motivated by a sense of awe and wonder in the face of the demonstrated demonic and angelic potential of the individual. At the same time we have the collective quest of a civilization, expressed individually through men and women made heroic by the wondrous adventure, to understand the mystery of the animal world, then the mystery of the dying and resurrecting plant world and—finally—the mystery of the heavenly world of the moon, the stars and the planets. And by the mid-1950s the two competing atomic powers, the United States and the Soviet Union, turned their attention to the exploration of this celestial terrain. The race for space was on.

In response to the Soviet Union's initial Space Age victory that saw them launch Sputnik, the first earth-orbiting satellite, on October 4, 1957, President John F. Kennedy, elected in 1960, vowed to send a man to the moon by the end of the decade. Kennedy's national challenge tapped into the adventurous spirit that fueled Western civilization's collective quest to explore and to understand the mysteries of our earthly world. Now, Kennedy said, the mysterious celestial world awaited us. He didn't live to see his vow fulfilled, having been assassinated on November 22, 1963, but by the end of the decade the 20th century explorer-heroes, Neil Armstrong and Buzz Aldrin, had eclipsed the Soviet Union's resounding Sputnik triumph. On July 20, 1969, they became the first human beings to set foot on the moon. And Armstrong took his "one small step for a man" but a "giant leap for mankind."

Until Western exploration of the earthly world began in earnest with the voyage of Christopher Columbus in 1492, our knowledge of the earth was limited to the biblical understanding authorized by the Church or to that expressed by the ancient Greeks. According to the Bible, the earth was flat, and while according to the ancient Greeks that same earth was round, it still was the stationary center of the known or imagined universe. In addition, our knowledge of the celestial world was reflected in the social order of the day expressed through the hierarchical structure of the Catholic Church and the empire it supported. As Joseph Campbell remarks in his essay "The Impact of Science on Myth" from his book 'Myths to Live By,' at the height of the Middle Ages:

> The Christian Empire was an earthly reflex of the order of the heavens, hieratically organized, with the vestments, thrones, and procedures of its stately courts inspired by celestial imagery, the bells of its cathedral spires and harmonies of its priestly choirs echoing in earthly tones the angelic hosts.

Thus the earthly voyages of Columbus and the explorers who were to follow him would severely test the accepted biblical image of the cosmos. And the continuing exploration of the celestial world, reflected in the work of the likes of Copernicus and Galileo, would threaten—and finally disprove—the seriously considered, ancient Greek notion of the round earth as the stationary center of the universe.

Without a doubt 1492 is a pivotal year in the history of Western civilization, so pivotal in fact that Mr. Campbell states in his same essay concerning the impact of science on myth:

> I like to think of the year 1492 as marking the end—or at least the beginning of the end—of the authority of the old mythological systems by which the lives of men had been supported and inspired from time out of mind.

If the year 1492 marks the beginning of the end of the "authority of the old mythological systems," then the year 1969, and specifically July 20, 1969, marks the final end of that authority and thus, for the Christian West, the final end of its Mythological Age. Finally, after almost 500 years of exhaustive exploration of our earthly terrain, we had journeyed 250,000 miles into our celestial terrain. And as a result of the journey, we had failed to discover any celestial God authorized by the "mythological system" that helped support the voyage in the first place.

The "mythological system" that "supported" and "inspired" the exploration of our earthly and celestial terrain was, of course, Christianity, with the Church supplying institutional enforcement. Initially, the Church enforced its "mythological system" from the papal throne in Rome and then, following the Protestant Reformation, from a variety of pulpits acting in opposition to that throne as well as to each other. From the early days of one Christian, or Catholic, Church to the latter days of a multitude of Christian churches, each claiming authenticity as The One True Church of Christ, the individual always grew to supposed maturity under the shadow of one of the various pulpits or of the singular papal throne. Although the various, authentic Christian churches doctrinally and catechetically opposed one another, they agreed on the most fundamental of all Christian premises. They agreed and held fast to the fundamental Christian teaching of "mythic dissociation."

Christopher Columbus' discoveries, as well as those of succeeding explorers, may have disproved accepted biblical notions concerning the shape of the earth, but they didn't seriously threaten, nor actually disprove, the fundamental Christian belief in a God separate from His human creations. Even the discoveries of Copernicus and Galileo in the 16th and 17th centuries didn't disprove this authorized doctrine. Their scientific discoveries, concerning the nature of the universe and earth's relationship to it, disproved previously accepted biblical notions of a stationary earth, but those same discoveries offered no tangible, experiential evidence that would disprove, or at least seriously threaten, the doctrine holding to the existence of a separate, celestial God. It was left to the celestial explorers of the late 20th century, the Alan Shepards, John Glenns, Neil Armstrongs, and Buzz Aldrins, ironically inspired—at least in part—by the paradisal dream of their "mythological system," to provide Western individuals, unwittingly, with the actual experience needed to both threaten and finally disprove the universal Christian doctrine of "mythic dissociation"—and to shatter the mythologically inspired, motivating dream of a civilization.

Christianity, the West's "mythological system," as the Church authority defined it from its various pulpits and singular papal throne, relied on the doctrine of "mythic dissociation" to generate its affect power to inspire and command belief. And as long as we had not journeyed into the celestial realm of Christianity's dissociated God, we had no experiential evidence to refute, or to threaten, its claims. Thus that "mythological system" enjoyed affective life well into the 20th century, despite its obvious scientific inaccuracies concerning the nature of the earth and the universe. With the essential doctrine of "mythic dissociation" still safe, the words spoken from church pulpits and the symbols presented on its altars had the affect power to direct individual lives along the path of redemption and salvation. Furthermore, those words and symbols could inspire the Western individual to continue the journey outward toward seemingly endless frontiers. But the outward journey into the celestial frontier of space produced no heavenly throne occupied by a dissociated, heavenly God. And actual—not imagined—television pictures of the moon, transmitted through some technological miracle, had revealed no man and no green cheese but only a barren landscape more desolate than anything found on earth. With the subsequent loss of the doctrine of a dissociated God that, in turn, deflated the mythologically inspired dream of the Garden of Paradise, the Christian West had reached the inevitable end of its Mythological Age.

However, the end of the Mythological Age doesn't signal the end of the Western individual. It signals the end of an era—the end of the era of an affectively living "mythological system" as defined and imposed by authority. To hold fast to a "mythological system" built on a premise discredited by scientific discovery and actual human experience is to hold on to a superstition. According to Joseph Campbell, in words taken from 'The Masks of God: Creative Mythology, "the meaning of the word 'superstition' "Latin, superstare, 'to standover,' from stare, 'to stand,' plus super, 'over' is 'simply belief in something standing over,' as a vestige, from the past." The Christian doctrine of "mythic dissociation," when we see it in light of the July 20, 1969, moonwalk, is such a superstition. As a "superstition," as a "vestige from the past," that doctrine—and the "mythological system" it supports—no longer can generate what Mr. Campbell would call "spiritual value." Such an image insisted on as fact today, as Mr. Campbell continues in 'Creative Mythology,' suggests "not accord but disaccord, not only with the known facts of the universe, but also with the science and civilization facing those facts."

With its various pulpits and singular papal throne still authorizing a "mythological system" built on "mythic dissociation," the institutional church finds itself—admittedly or not—more in "disaccord" than in "accord" with "the known facts of the universe" as well as "with the science and civilization facing those facts." As a result, the mythological dimension is missing in contemporary Western life, even though ministers and priests continue to preach the merits of a "mythological system" whose major premise conflicts with scientific knowledge about the nature of the universe and most of all, after the moonwalk, with the Western individual's experiential knowledge of that same celestial terrain. With the end of the Mythological Age we have witnessed, in effect, the death of God as we've always known Him throughout our institutional Christian era. Without the possibility of authentic belief in the structuring principle of all human life, ours is a civilization of T. S. Eliot's "hollow men" living Jean-Paul Sartre's existential complaint that "everything indeed is permitted if God does not exist."

But we need not accept being "hollow" as our only alternative living in an era marked by the death of God as expressed by the traditional, or orthodox, reading of our "mythological system." To anyone even remotely familiar with the historical emergence of the human race, the fact that we are beings capable of wonder is obvious. That fact didn't escape the discerning eye of F. Scott Fitzgerald, for example, who writes in 'The Great Gatsby' about a Long Island that, in the Columbian era of earthly exploration, "flowered once for Dutch sailor's eyes":

> for a transitory, enchanted moment man must have held his breath in the presence of this continent, compelled into an aesthetic contemplation he neither understood nor desired, face to face for the last time in history with something commensurate to his capacity for wonder.

That same "capacity for wonder" propelled us to the moon just 45 years after the publication of 'The Great Gatsby.' And the vision of the earth that 'flowered' before the eyes of the celestial explorers had to be even more majestic than that which "flowered once for Dutch sailors' eyes." Clearly, the Dutch sailors' discovery of the "fresh, green breast of the New World" wasn't the "last time in history" that "man" would come "face to face with something commensurate to his capacity for wonder."

This "capacity for wonder" is unique to our human race, and the Western individual, having led the way to the discovery of new earthly worlds and to the exploration of already discovered celestial worlds, can most freely live in expression of it. As long as we live that capacity, we don't live "hollow" lives. In words attributed to Christ in our "mythological system" of Christianity, each individual can "remain as a child" to keep the mythological dimension of life alive. In the presence "of something commensurate with his capacity for wonder," we are "compelled into an aesthetic contemplation" we neither understand nor desire. We don't have to live "hollow" lives as a result of our triumphant celestial exploration and walk on the moon. We don't have to live as if "everything indeed is permitted if God does not exist." Our courageous exploration of the barren landscape of the once mysterious moon hasn't resulted in us coming "face to face for the last time in history with something commensurate to our (his) capacity for wonder."

In discussing this same "capacity" in "The Importance of Rites" taken from 'Myths to Live By,' Joseph Campbell refers to culture historian Leo Frobenius to point out that:

> it was first the animal world in its varying species that impressed mankind as a mystery, and that, in its character of admired neighbor, evoked the impulse to imitative identification. Next, it was the vegetable world and the miracle of the fruitful earth, wherein death is changed into life.

The "animal world, in its varying species" and the "vegetable world and the miracle of the fruitful earth," visible to the eyes of affected individuals, compelled true believers "into an aesthetic contemplation (s) they (he) neither understood nor desired." F. Scott Fitzgerald's Dutch sailors and our own celestial explorers, when we see them in relation to earlier "aesthetic contemplation" of the wonder of the animal and vegetable worlds, help support the contention that this "capacity for wonder" is natural to the human species. And to live that "capacity" is to "remain as a child"—thus keeping life's mythological dimension affectively alive in "aesthetic contemplation" that no one even has to understand or desire.

The bold exploration of our celestial terrain, which we collectively witnessed through the miracle of television, is the inevitable result of human beings, with the rise of Near Eastern civilization, turning their attention away from the animal and vegetable worlds and towards what Joseph Campbell refers to as "the mathematics of the seven moving cosmic lights." The Christian Empire that flourished in the pre-Columbian world gradually emerged as an "earthly reflex of the order of the heavens" with "the bells of its cathedral spires and harmonies of its priestly choirs echoing in earthly tones the unearthly angelic hosts." This structure of earthly imitation of celestial harmony began to dissolve with the discoveries of Columbus in 1492 and finally dissolved amidst the euphoria and triumph that marked Neil Armstrong's and Buzz Aldrin's—and humankind's—walk on the moon on July 20, 1969. With that moonwalk we were left with the thought that we had nothing left "commensurate to our (his) capacity for wonder." And left without anything "commensurate" to this capacity, an individual can cease to "remain as a child." We can regress into a state of a "hollow" existence and live in visible chaos as if "everything indeed is permitted" now that "God does not exist."

It's up to the Western individual to recapture that childlike vitality common to the species. After the moonwalk of July 20, 1969, it's up to us to discover "something commensurate" to our "capacity for wonder." As we continue to focus our attention on the discovered multitude of "cosmic lights," we also can focus our attention on ourselves for as Mr. Campbell indicates, as did Leo Frobenius before him, in "The Importance of Rites" from 'Myths to Live By':

> our most mysterious neighbor today is not the animal or the plant; nor is it any longer the heavenly vault with its wonderfully moving lights. Frobenius points out that we have demythologized those through our sciences, and that the center of mystery is now man himself; man as Thou; one's neighbor; not as "I" might wish him to be, or may imagine that I know and relate to him, but in himself, thus come, as a being of mystery and wonder.

Having boldly led the exploration of the wonders of our earthly and celestial terrain, Western individuals, after the moonwalk, can just as boldly lead the exploration of the wonders of our mythological terrain—now properly read as psychology and not misread as science, history or biography. And we can "remythologize," as opposed to "demythologize," our foundational "mythological system" of Christianity to help illuminate our path of exploration.

During the years of our Mythological Age we saw ourselves as being subordinate to, and therefore dependent on, the institutional authority that enforced our "mythological system." Thus the Mythological Age of the Christian West was the Age of the Institution as well. However, 20th century celestial exploration, emphatically celebrated by Armstrong's and Aldrin's 1969 moonwalk, signaled the end of both ages. It marked the end of "the authority of the old mythological systems" but the beginning of the authority of the new systems. In the "remythologized mythological system" of Christianity, for example, the emphasis shifts away from the enforcing institution to the creative individual. And the institution assumes the responsibility of illuminating that path of creativity with the hope that deserving individuals will accept the psychological independence the "remythologized" mythological system commands.

For Carl Jung, to "remythologize" is to read the mythological system of the Christian West "symbolically" as psychology and not literally as either science, history or biography. In 'The Undiscovered Self,' written in 1958, 11 years before the moonwalk, Dr. Jung issued the telling challenge of our continuing scientific era when he asked: "Is it not time that the Christian Mythology, instead of being wiped out, was understood symbolically for once?" In addition, as early as 1949 with the publication of 'The Hero with a Thousand Faces' Joseph Campbell points out that "mythology is psychology misread as biography, history, and cosmology" when it really is a "rich and eloquent document of the profoundest depths of human character." The celestial exploration of the 20th century, that continues to the present day, failed to discover any dissociated God and thus reinforces Mr. Campbell's conviction and underscores the urgent significance of Dr. Jung's challenging question. The mythological system that helped inspire us to explore our earthly and celestial terrain isn't dead. Instead, we have failed to give it the chance to live, affectively, as it was meant to in the first place. The end of our Mythological Age signals the end of the Age of the Mythology of Authority, but at the same time it marks the beginning of the Age of the Mythology of the Individual.

In the mythological system of the Christian West the crucifix gives primary, or "archetypal," expression to the Mythology of the Individual and its accompanying, mytholgocially inspired paradisal dream. As the functioning symbol of the Christian altar during our Mythological Age, the crucifix was not a "superstition." Rather, it affectively lived in support of the Mythology of Authority that, prior to our experiential exploration of our celestial terrain, suggested and supported "a sense of man in accord with the universe." Associated primarily with the Roman Catholic Church, the crucifix, given "spiritual value" in support and in definition of the Mythology of Authority, could function as what Mr. Campbell would term a "living mythic symbol" and work its inspirational magic "through the eyes to the listening heart." However, with the doctrine of "mythic dissociation" discredited as a result of individual experience with the "monstrous nature of life"—since reinforced by the discoveries of rational science—that same Mythology of Authority, that proclaims the separation of God and the individual, suggests "not accord but disaccord, not only with the known facts of the universe, but also with the science and civilization facing those facts." Thus the crucifix, when we see it as supporting the Mythology of Authority, is merely—like the mythology itself—"something 'standing over,' as a vestige, from the past."

The crucifix is, indeed, a "vestige of the past." But as a "mythic" symbol and not a Christian, "historical" or "biographical" symbol, it is a "vestige" from the primal past, from Dr. Jung's "archetypal" or "collective" past. As such it is a symbolic expression of the "profoundest depths of human character." The crucifix is the Christian symbol Jung refers to in 'The Undiscovered Self.' Because of the breakdown of our "mythological system" and its accompanying structure supported by the doctrine of "mythic dissociation," we find ourselves "dissociated," to use Jung's term, and in need of a "directing and ordering principle" that the Mythology of Authority no longer can supply. However, as Jung explains in 'The Undiscovered Self,' the Mythology of the Individual—and its crucifix—can fill the void:

> This is not to say that Christianity is finished. I am, on the contrary, convinced that it is not Christianity, but our conception of it, that has become antiquated in face of the present world situation. The Christian symbol is a living thing that carries in itself the seeds of further development.

Collectively, "our conception" of Christianity, as it lived during the years of our Mythological Age, always had been that of a Mythology of Authority with the crucifix, at best, being of value as a Christian, historical and biographical symbol of a dissociated God's love for His creation. Our collective "conception" of Christianity never was that of a Mythology of the Individual with the crucifix serving as a "mythic symbol" expressing the individual human being's capacity for love. In fact, as Jung indicates in 'The Undiscovered Self,' the churches always condemned such a "will to individuality" as being a manifestation of "heresy and spiritual pride." Ironically, however, this Mythology of the Individual always was celebrated on the Christian altar in unconscious opposition to the pulpit and even to the papal throne that authorized the altar celebration. The crucifix, as the central symbol of that celebration, touched "the profoundest depths" of any "listening heart" and challenged the affected individual to obey the dictates of that heart in disobedience to the dictates of the reformed pulpit or the established papal throne. What Columbus unwittingly began in 1492, Neil Armstrong and Buzz Aldrin just as unwittingly "finished" in 1969. Indeed, "our conception of Christianity" has become "antiquated," and "in face of the present world situation"—visible to any honest eyes—the authentic "conception" of Christianity has yet to be discovered.

At the end of our Mythological Age, "the end of the authority of the old mythological systems," we can turn our attention inward not to discover a new mythological system but to discover, instead, a fresh understanding of our old system that helped inspire us to explore our earthly and celestial terrain in search of paradise always thought to be "out there" someplace. But as Dr. Jung points out in 'The Undiscovered Self' once again:

> Christianity holds at its core a symbol which has for its content the individual way of life of a man, the Son of Man, and that it even regards this individuation process as the incarnation and revelation of God himself.

According to the Mythology of Authority, built on the premise of "mythic dissociation," God is an anthropomorphic being separate from His human creation. But according to the Mythology of the Individual, God is a psychic being inherent in human beings, and the crucifix is a symbolic expression of this being that knows no sex and has no distinct personality, or life, separate from that of the individual. Inspired by the Christian altar celebration to obey the dictates of his "listening heart," the affected individual—unconsciously—was an "incarnation" and "revelation of God himself." After the moonwalk—after Neil Armstrong's "giant leap for mankind"—and at the end of our Mythological Age, we can explore our mythological, psychological terrain as boldly as we explored our earthly and celestial terrain to discover and live, consciously, that which we once had the chance to discover and live unconsciously.

As a result of our triumphant moonwalk, we have witnessed the end of a mythological way of life built on the authoritative premise of "mythic dissociation." Thus we have lost the motivating dream that gives life vitality and dignity and allows an individual, at least unconsciously, to "remain as a child" living in obedience to the experiential dictates of the crucified Hero of our mythological system. However, as Western individuals, we are but a part of the historical emergence of the human race, and as Mr. Campbell explains in 'The Masks of God: Creative Mythology':

> The rise and fall of civilizations in the long, broad course of history can be seen to have been largely a function of the integrity and cogency of their supporting canon of myth; for not authority but aspiration is the motivator, builder, and transformer of civilizations.

The aftermath of the moonwalk has left Western civilization, and the individuals who comprise it, in need of transformation. The "supporting canons" of our "myth" have lost their "integrity and cogency." And with the subsequent death of our motivating dream, we can live without "aspiration," at least unconsciously, in disobedience to the experiential dictates of the crucified Hero of our seemingly discredited mythological system.

But the Mythology of the Individual, embracing the crucifix as its primary, motivating symbol, is not discredited. Its premise of "mythic association," the union of the individual and God as the fundamental "canon" of the "myth," has "integrity and cogency" and therefore can provide the "aspiration" that is the "motivator, builder, and transformer of civilizations." The Mythology of the Individual, built on the premise of "mythic association," unlike the Mythology of Authority, built on that of "mythic dissociation," is not separate from life. Rather, it functions as an expression of a way of life. The Mythology of the Individual gives concrete expression to a way of life that leads to authentic maturity and psychological independence of the individual whose "profoundest depths" are revealed to be love rather than sin. And those "depths" are symbolically manifested in the mythology's Hero whose death results from a life of sacrifice. The crucified Hero of the Christian Mythology of the Individual lives not in accord with his will to pleasure or to power, as does the Pharisaic authority that opposes him, but in accord with his will to love which is the essence of him and thus of the individual, male or female without distinction or discrimination. By living in obedience to our will to love, the Hero, wearing one of a "thousand faces," achieves "individuation" and, in the process, lives as a symbolic expression of every individual's potential to live as an "incarnation and revelation of God himself."

When we read it as a Mythology of the Individual—as psychology—and not as a Mythology of Authority—as history or biography—the Christian Mythology can function not as something made up and therefore separate from experiential life but as something made up and therefore linked to that life instead. When we read it as a living Mythology of the Individual—as psychology—the Christian Mythology, through the image of its crucified Hero, celebrates the individual as a "being of mystery and wonder." It identifies the individual—living in obedience to the will to love as an "incarnation and revelation of God himself"—as the creative force in the universe. The Christian Mythology, when we read it creatively—as psychology—in support of a new Mythology of the Individual, can restore the mythological dimension, or "aspiration," to contemporary Western life. When we read it creatively, in accord with the scientific and experiential knowledge of our day, the Christian Mythology can provide the motivation we need to build and transform our civilization out of love for the universal individual whose community today no longer is the tribe, nation or even the civilization but, instead, the planet itself.

As Western individuals we stand at the threshold of our new Mythological Age of the Individual. If we can step across, we will allow ourselves to live, consciously, the experiential dictates of the Hero of our mythology. This new Mythological Age affords each of us the chance to live "as a child" in "aesthetic contemplation" of something we may neither understand nor desire but nonetheless still "face to face," this once and future time in our history, "with something commensurate to our capacity for wonder." Our fate on this planet rests in our own, individual hands. Both our life and our world, no longer protected by, or subjected to, any dissociated God, are now ours to destroy or to create. By living the sacrifice to be "an incarnation and revelation of God himself" we can create our own lives and contribute to the continuing creation of life on our planet. In discussing this "psychological sphere" of mythology, Joseph Campbell, once again in 'The Masks of God: Creative Mythology,' describes this particular function of an "adequate mythology" as:

> the centering and harmonization of the individual which in traditional systems was supposed to follow upon giving of oneself, and giving up of oneself altogether.

Mr. Campbell calls these "traditional systems," that demand the "giving up of oneself"—and thus the suppression of the individual—"reactionary systems" and identifies "the old Levantine one of the social order" as still "the most powerful today."

Such "Levantine systems," the Christian Mythology of Authority being one of them, no longer are "adequate" in the years and decades following our triumphant moonwalk when our explorer heroes—accompanied by millions who joined in the adventure through the magic of television—surveyed the earth from the heavens 250,000 miles away. A mythological system no longer in "accord" with scientific knowledge, and no longer in similar "accord" with the evidence of human experience, cannot "harmonize the individual." But any mythological system, the Christian Mythology of the Individual being one of them, that gives the individual the opportunity to live as "an incarnation and revelation of God himself" can accomplish that feat. Though once "adequate" in its call for the suppression of the individual, the old "Levantine system," reflected in the Christian Mythology of Authority, is now obsolete in an adventurous era that eventually gave birth to 20th century, manned celestial exploration. In discussing the obsolescence of "reactionary systems," and in support of his own conviction, Mr. Campbell—in 'Creative Mythology'—cites Dr. Loren Eiseley, whom he acknowledges as the author of a "lucid summary of the rise of modern science, 'The Firmament of Time': "The group ethic as distinct from personal ethic is faceless and obscure. It is whatever its leaders choose it to mean; it destroys the innocent and justifies the act in terms of the future." But, Mr. Campbell points our in referring to Dr. Eiseley's "warning," the "future is NOT the place to seek realization."

As obedient Western individuals we were "faceless and obscure" under the authority of our old mythological system. Therefore, we were obligated to suppress our individuality in the interests of preserving the social order that system created. As a result, we continued to journey outward in exploration of our earthly and celestial terrain, but we ignored the journey inward that leads to proper exploration of our mythological, psychological terrain. And our wondrous outward discoveries always were—and continue to be—justified "in terms of the future." According to Dr. Eiseley, such outward progress is "progress secularized." It is "progress which pursues only the next invention, progress which pulls thought out of mind and replaces it with idle slogans" and therefore is "not progress at all. It is a beckoning mirage in a desert over which stagger generations of men." In short, it is another expression of T. S. Eliot's "Waste Land" inhabited by "hollow men" living not "as a child" alive with awe and wonder but living instead Jean-Paul Sartre's complaint that "everything indeed is permitted if God does not exist." It is Eliot's "Waste Land" of "hollow men" living Sartre's existential despair masked by the glitter of Dr. Eiseley's "progress secularized."

Our new Mythological Age provides us with the "aspiration" that is "the motivator, builder, and transformer of civilizations" for as Dr. Jung expresses in 'The Undiscovered Self': "It is, unfortunately, only too clear that if the individual is not regenerated in spirit, society cannot be either, for society is the sum total of individuals in need of redemption." Having reached the end of our Mythological Age of Authority, we, as Western individuals, are in need of redemption. But we are not in need of redemption for having inherited Adam and Eve's original sin in authority's Garden of Eden. Instead, we are in need of enlightenment. And our mythological system, read as a creative Mythology of the Individual, provides us—in its crucifix—with a symbolic expression of that enlightenment and maturation. The crucified Hero of our Christian Mythology of the Individual provides us with a symbolic expression of the adult ego, of an individuated person living as an "incarnation and revelation of God himself." A society characterized by its "regenerated," individuated members is a society "regenerated in spirit" and one freed from slavery to a "hollow" existence living in a "Waste Land" of glitter devoid of any "directing and ordering principle."

The present is the time "to seek realization" and not the promised future as dictated by leaders of "reactionary systems." As long as we continue to measure progress only in terms of "the next invention," we will "stagger" over "a desert" along with other "generations of men." However, our new Mythological Age of the Individual, expressed in its crucifix which is "a living thing that carries in itself the seeds of further development," illuminates the way out of our desert "Waste Land." The Christian Mythology of the Individual, Jung's symbolic interpretation, commands individuals "to seek realization now." It is a command reinforced by Dr. Eiseley with whom Joseph Campbell concludes his chapter entitled "The Death of God" from 'Creative Mythology':

Because man, each individual man among us, possesses his own soul (Schopenauer's intelligible character) and by that light must live or perish, there is no way by which Utopias—or the lost Garden itself—can be brought out of the future and presented to man. Neither can he go forward to such a destiny. Since in the world of time every man lives but one life, it is in himself that he must search for the secret of the Garden.

And the "secret of the Garden" is manifested in the crucifix, in the individuated human being obedient to the will to love, living each individual's destiny as an "incarnation and revelation of God himself."

3

Existentialism: The Godless Philosophy of God

When we acknowledge ourselves as being a part of nature—rather than accepted as being apart from it—we prove to be more children of experience than children of authority. Therefore, our most fundamental laws, that structure and order our individual and collective existence, express the wisdom of that experience. We build this necessary structure and order around the concept of divinity that, in accord with experience, we can find everywhere in nature and thus in ourselves as part of—rather than apart from—that natural world. Pre-Christian, Western individuals could express this fundamental, experiential law through the language of mythology whose symbols, as Joseph Campbell reminds us in "The Confrontation of East and West in Religion" taken from 'Myths to Live By,' were then "left to speak for themselves—as rites, as works of art—through the eyes to the listening heart." The experiential, Natural Laws of the pre-Christian West, that acknowledged the presence of divinity in nature and thus in individual human beings, could be imprinted on each obedient, "listening heart" to direct an individual life along the way to maturity and union with the divinity. In our current, scientifically structured world these same, fundamental Laws of Nature find their expression in the modern philosophy of existentialism which, in turn, can generate the same directing power.

However, in our scientifically structured world existentialism does not enjoy the status of being acknowledged as A Philosophy of God let alone that of being accepted as The Philosophy of God. If existentialism enjoys any status at all in our modern world, it's that of being seen as The Godless Philosophy, making it—in either case—an anathema to any orthodox Christian thinker committed to preserving belief in God as the primary, structuring idea of human life. In 'Creative Mythology' Joseph Campbell poses the question: "do we not have among us in abundance today a species of philosophers who (maintaining in their own way the biblical notion that nature is corrupt) cannot discover in the nature either of man or of the universe any sign of inherent order?" The species of philosophers to whom Mr. Campbell refers is the existential species. And perhaps the most popularly known existentialist is Jean-Paul Sartre who, as the spokesman for that particular species, has to hold "the biblical notion that nature is corrupt."

In support of his question concerning this species of philosophers "in abundance today," Mr. Campbell points out that it is Sartre who:

> 'finds it extremely embarrassing that God does not exist; for there disappears with Him all possibility of finding values in an intellectual heaven.... Everything indeed is permitted if God does not exist, and man is in consequence forlorn; for he cannot find anything to depend upon either within or outside himself.... We are left alone, without excuse. That is what I mean when I say that man is condemned to be free.'

But Sartrean existentialism is based on the "biblical notion that nature is corrupt"—an idea unknown to the pre-Christian era where divinity lived in nature and in individual human beings, necessarily accepted as creatures of nature. Thus Sartrean existentialism is more a product of the questioning of biblical authority, and the supporting institutional church, than it is a product of the interpretation of natural, human experience. In our scientifically structured world, we, as Western individuals, have to journey beyond the boundaries of Sartrean thought to discover the authentic existentialism of experience that illuminated for our predecessors, and can illuminate for us as well, the way to discovery of and union with the divinity—the way to the discovery and union with God.

Our pre-Christian, pagan predecessors never heard of the doctrine of original sin, but because of the very nature of life they had to experience the Sartrean "absurd world" and its most fundamental conclusion—that all living things, human beings included, must die. In fact, we are unique among all the primates because as Joseph Campbell concludes in "The Emergence of Man" from 'Myths to Live By': "in this wonderful human brain of ours there has dawned a realization unknown to other primates. It is that of the individual, conscious of himself as such, and aware that he, and all that he cares for, will one day die." Mr. Campbell follows up this conclusion by saying "this recognition of mortality and the requirement to transcend it is the first great impulse to mythology." Thus human beings, in their primal awareness of the death of every individual member of their species, had to express, through the symbolic language of their mythology, a way of life that led to this transcendence and to union with the divinity. Moreover, because of the premise on which it was based, this way of life—this philosophy—had to be existential in nature. But unlike Sartrean existentialism, it had to be free from the "biblical notion that nature is corrupt.' Thus Sartrean existentialism cannot be the authentic existentialism of experience. Therefore, we cannot be "condemned to be free." Authentic existentialism, the philosophy of experience—free from the coercive influence of biblical, pulpit Christianity and its doctrine of original sin—has to celebrate freedom as being our destiny rather than our condemnation.

Western existentialism in the Sartrean mode is a philosophy of experience all right, but it is not The Philosophy of Experience. It is a Godless philosophy, as stated in Sartre's "complaint," only because it emerges as a result of our experience of conflict with the order and structure of the universe imposed by the biblical and dogmatic authority of the Christian church. To refer to William Faulkner and the appropriate descriptive language he employs in his novel, 'Absalom, Absalom!!' this imposed "Grand Design" cannot hold up in the face of the challenge posed either by accumulated experience with life or by the individual's developing capacity to reason. As a result, we can lose faith in that "Design" as well as in the authority that imposed it—thus the Sartrean lament that "man is condemned to be free." For the Sartrean existentialist man is "condemned to be free" in a Godless, "absurd world" because the existence of the God of the Christian authority presiding over the "Grand Design" cannot be supported by experience or by human reason. That "Design" then disintegrates as a result. Left alone with no God and with nothing "to depend upon either within or outside himself," the individual human being—male and female alike—"is in consequence forlorn." This state of alienation and meaninglessness where "everything indeed is permitted" is permanent only if there is no other "Grand Design" to discover. However, such a "Design" does exist. Thus the contemporary state of existential despair is a necessary step on our journey to maturation. It is a necessary step leading to the state of existential rapture that results from the discovery of the forgotten and discredited "Grand Design" that places the individual human being, at-one with nature and God, at its center.

To live as autonomous individuals in charge of our and, ultimately, the world's, salvation, we have to see ourselves as being free from the constraining influence of original sin. If we aren't free from its constraints, we have no autonomy because we remain dependent on the Church to supply the vehicle for God's grace without which neither us nor our world can be saved. In such a world individual autonomy cannot exist. In fact, to seek it is to fall victim to "hubris" or to live in a state of spiritual pride separate from God and His Church which provides the necessary source of our spiritual life. In a world structured around the doctrine of original sin we, as individuals, do not enjoy freedom. Furthermore, we are cut off from the salvatory power of any natural laws that have emerged as a result of authentic, existential human experience. In our contemporary, scientific world the doctrine of original sin is as obsolete as the "Grand Design" it supports. The historicity of that structure's facts has been refuted by the evidence of accumulated experience, the development of reason and the discoveries of rational science. We are left with the individual artist, who—consciously or unconsciously—always has been free from original sin, to illuminate the path of order that can lead us out of the inevitable chaos that characterizes life in our scientifically ordered world.

Sartre's vision is not the vision of the artist simply because it is not an all encompassing vision that transcends the boundaries defining the "Grand Design" of the Christian West built on the authoritative, rather than experiential, doctrine of original sin. Having reasoned beyond that concept and its erected boundaries, Sartre stops with his existential "complaint" that there is no God and, therefore, no hope for order in a chaotic universe where man is "condemned to be free." Sartre's vision is a "nihilistic" existential vision, but William Faukner expressed its "romantic" counterpart in his April 24, 1958, address to the English Club of the University of Virginia.

Faulkner's address, in part, was in response to President Dwight D. Eisenhower's plan of two years earlier to create a sense of order in a dangerous world made more so by what Faulkner identifies as "antagonistic and seemingly irreconcilable governments." In recognition of this "universal dilemma of mankind" President Eisenhower proposed, in Faulkner's words:

> that individual people in all walks of life should be given the opportunity to speak to their individual opposite numbers all over the earth—laborer to laborer, scientist to scientist, doctors and lawyers and merchants and bankers and artist to their opposite numbers everywhere.

To Faulkner "there was nothing wrong with this idea" because "trying to communicate to man regardless of race or color or condition is exactly what every artist has already spent his life trying to do, and as long as he breathes will continue to do so." What "doomed" the plan in Faulkner's assessment:

> was an evil inherent in our culture itself; an evil quality inherent in (and perhaps necessary though I for one do not believe this last) the culture of any country capable of enduring and surviving through this period of history. This

is the mystical belief, almost a religion, that individual man cannot speak to individual man because individual man can no longer exist.

President Eisenhower's plan to deal with a universally recognized problem was the plan of someone burdened by, and not free from, the authoritative doctrine of original sin. Faulkner's response, on the other hand, is that of an individual human being—of an artist—freed from that sin and its visionary constraints.

President Eisenhower's vision was neither "nihilistic" nor "romantic." If anything, it was an "idealistic" vision based not on the integrity of the autonomous individual but rather on that of the group to which the individual surrenders that autonomy. It is a vision based more on obedience to the laws of the group rather than to the laws of universal, human experience. To the "romantic" existential thinker, convinced that the integrity of the individual is a sacred and fundamental fact of human experience, such a vision is doomed. In his ultimate response to President Eisenhower's idealistic proposal, colored by the president's adherence to the doctrine of original sin, Faulkner confirms his own—and the artist's—romance and freedom from that same doctrine:

> So in the case—I mean the President's People-to-People Committee—the artist too, who has already spent his life trying to communicate simply people to people the problems and passions of the human heart and how to survive them or anyway endure them, has in effect been asked by the President of his country to affirm that mythology which he has already devoted his life to denying: the mythology that one single individual man is nothing, and can have weight and substance only when organized into the anonymity of a group where he will have to surrender his soul for a number.

The mythology to which Faulkner refers and to which he says the artist "has already devoted his life to denying," is that which imposed on the individual a world order, a "Grand Design," structured around the doctrine of original sin. On the other hand, the mythology that he and the artist must devote their lives to supporting would be one that creates for the individual a world order, a "Grand Design," free from the structuring influence of that same doctrine. According to the "traditional" order, supported by the original sin doctrine, salvation depends upon the individual surrendering "his individual soul for a number." According to the "creative" order, supported by the existential law recognizing the divinity inherent in nature and humankind, salvation depends upon the individual discovering and living that divinity. In effect, such discovery and commitment leads to the creation of a world order, a "Grand Design," dominated by responsible individuals obedient to the universal laws of nature. Having reasoned beyond the doctrinaire, Christian idealism of President Eisenhower and beyond the existential nihilism of Jean-Paul Sartre, William Faulkner—the artist—discovers the romance, and thus the divinity, that lives within us all as equal expressions of the authentic, existential individual.

The Christian idealism reflected in President Eisenhower's proposal of 1956 owes its life to the fundamental Christian premise of "mythic dissociation," as does the existential nihilism reflected in Sartre's "complaint." In reference to Sartre, however, the individual has lost faith in that authoritative doctrine. The existential romance reflected in Faulkner's address to the English Club of the University of Virginia is born from "mythic dissociation" as well, but Faulkner's romance carries the individual beyond the boundaries of its nihilistic counterpart—thus completing the cycle of maturation that, ironically, reinforces the vision of Pelagius, a fifth-century contemporary to St. Patrick and St. Augustine, the orthodox champions.

The Christian idealist holds fast to his church as the vehicle of God's grace to which any individual must "surrender his soul" while the existential nihilist is separated from that church and abandoned in a "Godless world where he cannot discover in the nature either of man or the universe any sign of inherent order." But, as Joseph Campbell explains in 'The Masks of God: Creative Mythology,' Pelagius taught neither Christian idealism, based on the integrity of the group to which the individual surrenders his soul, nor existential nihilism, based on the "complaint" that there is no God and thus no "inherent order" in the universe:

> Pelagius and his followers absolutely rejected the doctrine of our inheritance of the sin of Adam and Eve, and taught that we have finally no need of supernatural grace; no need of a miraculous redemption, but only of awakening and maturation; and that though the Christian is advantaged by the model and teachings of Christ, every man is finally (and must be) the author and means of his own fulfillment.

Because Pelagius "absolutely rejected the doctrine of our inheritance of the sin of Adam and Eve," he could not accept the orthodox idea of God, as a being separate from the individual, that is built on that doctrine. In disagreement with the existential nihilists, "maintaining in their own way the biblical notion that nature is corrupt," and in agreement with the existential romantics who defend the inherent dignity and integrity of the individual, Pelagius taught that our "nature itself is full of grace." That which the eyes of orthodox authority see as heresy ends up reinforcing Faulkner and the vision of the artist with its acceptance of the most fundamental of all experiential laws proclaiming that divinity exists as part of, rather than apart from, nature and, necessarily, as part of the individual human being as well.

Thus the fifth-century Pelagian heresy reinforces the 20th-century romantic existentialism of the artist clearly expressed, and defended, by William Faulkner in his address to the English Club of the University of Virginia in 1958. In the process this Pelagian heresy connects the 20th-century vision of the artist with the Western individual's pre-Christian, pagan past, giving it—as seen through the eyes of orthodox authority still holding fast to the "doctrine of our inheritance of the sin of Adam and Eve"—the same heretical status. Judged in relation to the scientific "facts" of the biblical authority on which the institutional church is based, both Pelagius and Faulkner would have to be condemned as heretics. However, judged in relation to the scientific "facts" of modern, rational inquiry, the Church suffers that condemnation. With its "doctrine of our inheritance of the sin of Adam and Eve" discredited by rational, scientific facts that deny the historicity of the Garden of Eden story, the Church—as long as it holds fast to that doctrine—cannot offer its followers any authentic hope for either individual or collective salvation. The facts of rational science vindicate, and support, the Pelagian heresy and proclaim, at the same time, the rational, romantic existential vision of the artist to be the salvatory vision of the Western individual. Jean-Paul Sartre's world may be "absurd," but we are not to fear it. Instead, we are to celebrate it as being a great and noble world because human beings can achieve greatness and nobility within it.

We can achieve such status within this "absurd world" because we can discover—and live—the "grace," the divinity, our nature is "full of." In the history of the Christian West this grace, this existential essence of the individual, is first given concrete expression in what Joseph Campbell identifies as the "courtly cult of Amor." This "cult" of love emerged in the 12th and 13th centuries fed by the still not forgotten Celtic, pagan mythologies throughout which, Mr. Campbell says, "there is an essential reliance on nature, as in all great mythologies." Thus the medieval "courtly cult of Amor," that celebrates the individual as being naturally "full of grace," existed in direct contrast to orthodox authority where "according to every churchly doctrine, nature had been so corrupted by the Fall of Adam and Eve that there was no virtue in it whatsoever." Thus to obey this existential romance a medieval individual had to disobey established, orthodox authority. In effect, a person had to, referring to Mr. Campbell once again, "challenge Hell." But in so doing the individual, "as though moved by an infallible "NATURAL grace, follows without fear the urges of his heart." In consequence he or she can "communicate to a life, if not the radiance of eternal life, at least integrity and truth."

In the eyes of orthodox authority the essence of this heart is sin, a conclusion consistent with "the doctrine of our inheritance of the sin of Adam and Eve." Thus that same authority does not recognize Amor but instead recognizes Agape, what Mr. Campbell refers to as "an indiscriminate Love feast," of the "charitable, church supper type," as the ultimate expression of Christian love. Furthermore, orthodox authority, holding fast to its "doctrine of our inheritance of the sin of Adam and Eve," proclaims Christ as being the ultimate, heroic expression of the Agape lover, thus providing the "role model" for all believing Christians to follow. In the eyes of the existential nihilist, who has reasoned to the conclusion that the world is Godless, the celebration of Agape—with Christ cast in the role of its ultimate expression—is useless. He or she is left with Eros, another "indiscriminate Love feast" that Mr. Campbell refers to as being of the "orgiastic variety," as opposed to the "charitable church supper type." Thus the existential romantic—the artist as a child of nature—is left to recognize, and to celebrate, Amor as the concrete expression of that "grace" that our individual nature is "full of," as the concrete expression of the divinity that resides in the individual "heart."

Keeping with the analysis of love Mr. Campbell offers in 'The Masks of God: Creative Mythology,' Amor, unlike Agape and Eros, is "discriminate." Also, it "follows the lead and allure of the senses, and in particular the noblest sense, that of sight." In the "courtly cult of Amor," celebrated in the lyrics of the Medieval troubadours, "we hear little or nothing of the fall and corruption either of the senses or of the world." Thus Amor is set apart from either the Agape or Eros "Love Feast" where the "whole point" of such a celebration "and the very virtue of communal love, is that its aim is indiscriminate. 'Love the neighbor as thyself.'" Continuing with his analysis of the contrast between the "discriminate" Amor and the "indiscriminate" Agape and Eros, Mr. Campbell adds:

> Selectivity, the prime function of the eyes and heart, is in the Agape methodically abjured. The lights go out so to say, and whatever is at hand, one loves—either in the angelic way of charity or in the orgiastic, demonic way of the Dionysian orgy; but in either case, religiously in renunciation of ego, ego judgment, and ego choice.

To the believing, orthodox Christian, holding to the "doctrine of our inheritance of the sin of Adam and Eve," loving in the "angelic way of charity" is directly opposed to loving in the "demonic way of the Dionysian orgy." As Mr. Campbell explains, the former—"charity"—is seen as being "godly and spiritual of men toward each other in a community and the latter—'lust'—natural and fleshly, being the urge, desire, and delight of sex." Mr. Campbell exclaims that "it is amazing, but our theologians still are writing of Agape and Eros and their radical opposition, as though these two were the final terms of the principle of 'love.'" To the orthodox Christian, still burdened by the authoritative doctrine of original sin, no other term referring to the "principle of love" can exist. And the existentialist nihilist cannot know love, only despair, because "God does not exist" and the individual "has nothing to depend on either within or outside himself." Only the romantic existentialist—the artist—knows of Amor, even if he or she hasn't heard the term, "as a third, selective, discriminating principle in contrast to the other two."

To the romantic existentialist—to the artist—whether expressed in the fifth-century Pelagian heresy or in Faulkner's 20th-century address to the English Club of the University of Virginia, God does exist. And this God is neither Agape nor Eros but Amor that "nobody in the pulpit seems to have heard of" and that nobody in that existential "species of philosophers" seems ever to have heard of either. This Amor, this God, repeatedly is manifested in art that celebrates neither:

> the right hand path (the sublimating spirit, the mind and community of man), nor the indiscriminate left (the spontaneity of nature, the mutual incitement of the phallus and the womb). but is the path directly before one, of the eyes and their message to the heart.

This "path directly before one" is the path illuminated "in all great pagan mythologies" where "there is throughout an essential reliance on nature." It is the path of the authentic Hero, "the Hero with a thousand faces," who, "as though moved by an infallible NATURAL grace, follows without fear the urges of his heart." The authentic Hero (Huckleberry Finn provides a classic example for the American reader. See Chapter One.), regardless of appearance or "face," follows the "urges of his heart" and not the authoritative doctrine of any group that expects the surrendering of one's soul. And the Hero is not "forlorn" or "condemned to be free" because in following the "urges of his heart" such an individual is living God with or without any conscious realization. In this "essential reliance on nature," as opposed to reliance on authority, the Hero lives each individual's destiny to be free—suffering no condemnation in that regard.

To the romantic existentialist—the artist—having broken free from the "doctrine of our inheritance of the sin of Adam and Eve," Christ—the orthodox authority's role model—emerges as one expression of "the Hero with a thousand faces." He emerges as the Hero, unique only in his "face," because "he follows without fear the urges of his heart." Thus to the romantic existentialist the Christian Mythology affirms the pagan mythologies in their own celebration of the Hero following the "urges of his heart" and "moved by an infallible NATURAL grace." In this Christian affirmation of the pagan mythologies, Christ as Hero emerges as the symbolic expression of Amor and not as the ultimate "role model" for Agape. The Amor lover, the Hero, does not surrender his or her soul to any vehicle of grace because his or her own nature, and thus the nature of all individuals, already is "full of grace." An individual human being, therefore, has "no need for miraculous redemption, but only of awakening and maturation" which precisely is the illuminated path of "all great pagan mythologies" subsequently affirmed by the equally great Christian Mythology.

If we experience the nihilistic "complaint" and the subsequent condemnation "to be free," we only take a necessary step on the way to "awakening and maturation." We have to experience the death of the God of orthodox authority in order to discover the authentic God who resides within the individual heart and is repeatedly expressed through the Hero in previously discredited "pagan mythologies." The Medieval individual had to have the courage to "challenge Hell" to follow "without fear the urges of his heart." But contemporary individuals no longer face that challenge. With "the doctrine of our inheritance of the sin of Adam and Eve" discredited by our own application of reason and the subsequent scientific discoveries, that Hell—whose existence depends upon the infallibility of that doctrine—is discredited as well. As a result, we are free from the reality of that earlier fear and thus free to discover the essence of the human heart. We are free to discover the way to individual and collective "awakening and maturation." Living in the shadow of rational, scientific inquiry, we must confront a much more immediate Hell if we fail to answer the call.

The Hell that the Medieval individual had to challenge in order to be free no longer burdens us because the "doctrine of our inheritance of the sin of Adam and Eve" is as obsolete as the order and structure it supports. But contrary to Sartre's "complaint" that "everything indeed is permitted if God does not exist," everything is not permitted because God does exist as what Dr. Jung terms a "psychic being" that, once awakened, demands to be obeyed. Disobeying that call of Amor, disobeying the "urges of one's heart," leads to experiencing the psychic pain of Hell that is more real—and more immediate—than the Hell created by a separate God—the "prison house" as James Joyce refers to it in his 'Portrait of the Artist as a Young Man'—to house, among others, any individual who "as though moved by an infallible NATURAL grace, follows without fear the urges of his heart."

When we view it with eyes freed from the "doctrine of our inheritance of the sin of Adam and Eve" and thus "having no need for a miraculous redemption," the crucifix, symbolically and quietly, illuminates the path of the "heart"—the path of "awakening and maturation," the path of the autonomous individual who is "the author and means of his own fulfillment." It illuminates the path of the Hero, the path of Amor, the romantic existential path of discovery and union with the authentic God that dwells within every individual whose "nature itself is full of grace." It is the path "directly before one, of the eyes and their message to the heart." It is the path that leads to the state of existential rapture that results from discovering the forgotten and discredited "Grand Design" of the "great pagan mythologies" with the autonomous individual in union with God at the center. To "follow the urges of his heart" the medieval Christian had to face "The ultimate disaster of Hell for all eternity" but not so for us. We face the immediate "disaster" of psychic pain and despair—the existential Hell to be experienced in this immediate world if we fail to answer the call of Amor—that "path directly before one, of the eyes and their message to the heart." In answering the call of Amor, symbolically expressed in the crucifix, the contemporary individual "communicates to a life" not just "integrity and truth" but "the radiance of eternal life" as well.

As did our pre-Christian, pagan predecessors, we need a reason for our existence. The romantic existential vision of the artist—expressed in "all great pagan mythologies," the Pelagian reading of the Christian Mythology, and repeated in Faulkner's address to the English Club of the University of Virginia in 1958—provides us with that reason. We need only to practice our romantic existential religion that assigns us the importance and responsibility we deserve as revealed in the words of Ochwaiy Biano, the Pueblo Indian whom Dr. Jung quotes in his chapter entitled "Travels" from 'Memories, Dreams, and Reflections':

> 'After all,' he said, 'we are all people who live on the roof of the world; we are the sons of the Father Sun, and with our religion we daily help our Father to go across the sky. We do this not only for ourselves, but for the whole world. If we were to cease practicing our religion, in ten years the sun would no longer rise. Then it would be night forever.'

Released from the visionary constraints of original sin, we are now free to discover our religion and just as free to practice it not only for ourselves but "for the whole world." Ochwaiy Biano, speaking for the Pueblo Indian, understood that if he did not practice his religion, "it would be night forever."

Addressing the issue of the importance of the individual and the accompanying responsibility, Dr. Jung continues in 'Memories, Dreams, and Reflections,' echoing the convictions Faulkner expressed in his address to the English Club of the University of Virginia:

> He himself (individual man) is the second creator of the world, who alone has given to the world its objective existence—without which, unheard, unseen, silently eating, giving birth, dying, heads nodding through hundreds of millions of years, it would have gone on in the profoundest night of non-being to its unknown end. Human consciousness created objective existence and meaning, and man found his indispensable place in the great process of being.

No longer burdened by the "doctrine of our inheritance of the sin of Adam and Eve," we are free to discover our "indispensable place in the great process of being" which was then, is now and always will be at the center, living our existential majesty in union with the experiential, universal God of Amor—that "infallible NATURAL grace" that resides within the "heart" as the existential essence of the individual human being.

4

The Heart of Rock n' Roll

Our knowledge of death sets us apart from the other creatures of nature, and as we have seen, this knowledge—and the need to transcend it—supplies us with the necessary motivation to create mythology. With it we help to remind ourselves that "there is more to life than death," to borrow a memorable line from a relatively obscure—but nonetheless evocative—1982 Australian, "coming of age" movie, 'The Man from Snowy River.' In one or another of its various expressions, mythology is as old as civilized human beings with the beginning of the era of civilization being associated with what Joseph Campbell terms in 'The Way of the Animal Powers' "the awakening of awe." In this first volume of his four volume 'Historical Atlas of World Mythology' Mr. Campbell dates the origins of life on earth as being some "31/2 billion years ago, in the briny oceans of our planet" and goes on to say that:

> the innocence of Eden had prevailed until, at some point in time, the eyes which along the lines of animal life had evolved as agents of the quest for nourishment were opened to a dimension within, beyond, and behind what in India is termed 'the sheath of food,' the tangible, visible forms of phenominality.

That "point in time," Mr. Campbell continues, "can only have been at some unrecorded moment in the course of the last "31/2 <u>million</u> years" when "in the human line the crisis occurred of the awakening to the mystery of death." With this "awakening of awe" humankind began to express, through mythology, not the way to eliminate or to avoid death—which, without the cause-effect influence of the doctrine of original sin, had to be natural—but the way to live with its necessary reality in transcendence of it. Various mythological forms, that continued to evolve with the human species, expressed what the eyes saw as the "dimension within, beyond, and behind what in India is termed 'the sheath of food.'" Music is but one of these forms that, essentially, are products of the eyes which—as

Shakespeare tells us about the poet—can give "to airy nothingness a local habitation and a name." And by the mid-20th century, revealed through the innovative musical form of rock n' roll, Western eyes—specifically American in this case—had identified and celebrated love as that "dimension within, beyond, and behind what in India is termed 'the sheath of food.'"

We can divide the life of the musical form of rock n' roll into two separate eras—its 'Rock Around the Clock' era covering the years from 1954 to 1965 and its 'Satisfaction' era covering the years from 1965 to the beginning of the 21st century and seemingly beyond. The two eras are distinct from each other in both style and content. Citing Joseph Campbell's reference to "Nietzsche's statements regarding classic and romantic art"—"The Importance of Rites" from 'Myths to Live By'—rock n' roll's 'Rock Around the Clock' era provides us with an example of "the romanticism of true power that shatters contemporary forms to go beyond these to new forms." In contrast, its 'Satisfaction' era provides us with an example of "the romanticism that is unable to achieve form at all and so smashes and disparages out of resentment." In the fresh, developing years of rock n' roll we had nothing as yet to disparage or resent, making the flamboyant antics of its Little Richards innocent in comparison to the more disparaging and resentful antics of its high tech, heavy metal successors. But the early years of the 1960s, highlighted by the Second Vatican Council of the authoritative Roman Catholic Church that convened in 1962 and concluded in 1965, witnessed the questioning—and the subsequent waning of the power and influence—of institutional authority in general. As a result, the troubadour spirit of love, "the dimension within, beyond, and behind 'the sheath of food,'" gave way to the rebellious spirit of chaos that "smashes and disparages out of resentment."

With nothing to disparage or resent, the performers of rock n' roll's 'Rock Around the Clock' era were free to celebrate, in their "new form" which had powerfully shattered "contemporary forms," the magic and mystery of love. Without their conscious knowledge, these performers—with names like Ricky, Buddy, Jimmy, Frankie and even Elvis—provided their youthful audience with a link to the Western world's pre-Christian past. Still unconscious of their role, of course, they were 20th century expressions of the minstrels of pagan lore, particularly—as we learn from 'The Masks of God: Creative Mythology'—"the pagan Celtic lore of Ireland, Cornwall, and Wales." As we learn in that same work: "The Celtic myths and legends are full of tales of singers and harpers of the fairy hills whose music has the power to make men weep, to make men sleep, and to make men laugh." In addition, they appear mysteriously from "the land of Eternal Youth, the land of the Fairy Hills, the Land below Waves." With nothing to disparage or resent, the Ricky Nelsons, Buddy Hollys, and Elvis Presleys—"singers and harpers of the Fairy Hills"—appeared "mysteriously from the Land of Eternal Youth" singing their songs of the mystery of love which alone has the power "to make men weep, to make men sleep, and to make men laugh."

But the decade of the 60s marked the beginning of the Age of Disparagement and Resentment that continues into the 21st century. The last "singers and harpers of the Fairy Hills" to appear "mysteriously from the Land of Eternal Youth" were The Beatles, Buddy Holly and the Crickets in page-boy haircuts, singing 'I Saw Her Standing There' and 'I Want to Hold Your Hand.' Like their American predecessors, The Beatles had nothing to disparage or resent. It was left to The Rolling Stones, with their complaint of "can't get no satisfaction," to break with the heritage of "pagan Celtic lore"—with its "singers and harpers of the Fairy Hills"—and transform rock n' roll from an inspiring expression of the "romanticism of true power that shatters contemporary forms to go beyond these to new forms" into a despairing expression of "the romanticism that is unable to achieve form at all, and so smashes and disparages out of resentment." With this transformation rock n' roll lost its heart. It lost sight of the troubadour spirit of love, "the music of the Land below Waves," whose "singers and harpers" from the age of the lyre to that of the electric guitar, from the pagan minstrels to The Beatles, celebrated its mysterious power to "enchant and to move the world."

Whereas the pagan minstrels from the days of "Celtic lore" had no authority contrary to the laws of nature with which to contend, the original Christian troubadours from the 12th and 13th centuries had the Church of Rome. From its papal throne and from its pulpits, the Church condemned nature as being corrupt and with its subsequent separation of God and His creations, celebrated Heaven—and not earth—as being what Joseph Campbell in 'Creative Mythology' refers to as "the true domain of love." To the Church the "corruption ruinous of love" was nature. Consequently, it turned its attention to its celestial Heaven and to its God separate from humankind, corrupted, like nature itself, by the sin of Adam and Eve in the Garden of Paradise. To the "singers and harpers" of "pagan Celtic lore," however, neither nature nor humankind was corrupt. They had not heard of any corrupting sin in any garden paradise, nor had they heard of any eternal fires of Hell that awaited any individual who disobeyed God's doctrine expressed through His Church. The pagan "singers and harpers" appeared from the "Fairy Hills" of nature and for them divinity was immanent, as opposed to transcendent, in all things. Thus, as Mr. Campbell indicates in his volume of 'Creative Mythology,' they sang of the "hidden Being of beings particularly in certain heroic individuals, who thus stand as epiphanies of that 'manifest hidden' which moves and lives within us all and is the secret of the harmony of nature."

To the "singers and harpers" of "pagan Celtic lore," then, the "corruption ruinous of love" was not nature. On the contrary, individuals turned to nature for inspiration in a life so mysterious and majestic as to include death. Out of the "Fairy Hills" came the secret of the mystery of life and the transcendence of death. The "singers and harpers" of medieval lore, the troubadours, in opposition to their Church of Rome and in accord with their counterparts of "pagan Celtic lore," saw "this blossoming earth" and "not heaven" as "the true domain of love as it is of life." Therefore, "the corruption ruinous of love was not of nature (of which love is the very heart) but of society, both lay and ecclesiastical; the public order and, most importantly, its sacramentalized, loveless marriages." The Church, of course, casting its eyes toward Heaven, "sacramentalized loveless marriages" and condemned the love celebrated by the troubadours as immoral. As a result, it helped set the stage for the later condemnation of such love, directed toward the domain of earth here and now, as being merely "puppy love." The afflicted individual had to outgrow this stage of youthful ignorance in order to grow into the adult vision that embraced marriage as the end, or purpose, of an individual life. The Church continued to "sacramentalize" loveless marriages, and society continued to discourage the immature "puppy love" of "this blossoming earth," reinforcing the conviction of the troubadour spirit that identified "society, both lay and ecclesiastical" and not "nature" as "the corruption ruinous of love."

In opposition to the Church of Rome (Roma) the love celebrated by the medieval troubadours became known as Amor. It was love of "this blossoming earth" awakened, and not corrupted, by nature "of which love is the very heart." And the singers of its song were messengers from the "Fairy Hills," from the mysterious "Land below Waves" that serious explorers of the human psyche—such as Carl Jung—might see as the depths of the unconscious. In reference to this "Land below Waves," the individual's unconscious identity—the pagan, Celtic "hidden Being of beings" or the "dimension behind 'the sheath of food'"—would be Amor whose song, created in response to what Sartre would see as the "absurd world," is one of immortality in transcendence of death. Because the Amor message from the "singers and harpers" is that of nature, it is love born in the senses not corrupted by any sin in any garden paradise. As humankind knew with the "awakening of awe," as Shakespeare knew in musing about the poet and as Joseph Campbell reminds us in 'Creative Mythology' "the noblest sense" is "that of sight." Accordingly, Amor is born in the eyes and travels directly to the heart or to the depths of the unconscious "Land below Waves" that Jung found to be "collective."

To the Church of Rome in the 12th and 13th centuries, given its doctrine of original sin and its subsequent insistence on the separation of God and the individual in opposition to the experiential vision of "pagan Celtic lore," the heart—or unconscious—had to be sin. If the Church were to acknowledge a "collective unconscious," it would see it as being collectively sinful and would identify itself—the Church of the One, True God—as the only authentic vehicle for redemption and salvation. Unlike their pagan predecessors who did not have to contend with the effects of any original sin, the troubadours had to sing a song in opposition to the established ecclesiastical authority that in turn influenced, and dominated, the thinking of lay authority. To live the song of the troubadours, directed not toward the institutional Heaven but toward "this blossoming earth," the medieval individual had to disobey both the lay and ecclesiastical worlds. Obedience to those authorities would prove ruinous to the very love whose song held "the power to enchant and move the world."

By the mid-20th century, the era of the birth of rock n' roll, that same Church, now split into various factions with each claiming authenticity, still held fast to its doctrine of original sin and its subsequent insistence on the separation of God and the individual. Furthermore, if it were to acknowledge a "collective unconscious," it still would see it as being collectively sinful and still would identify the now split and divided Church as the only authentic vehicle for redemption and salvation. The 20th century troubadours, therefore, had to sing a song—like their medieval counterparts but unlike their pagan predecessors—in opposition to the established ecclesiastical authority that still influenced, and dominated, lay authority. To live, consciously or unconsciously, the song of the troubadours—still directed away from the institutional Heaven and toward "this blossoming earth"—the 20th century individual had to disobey both ecclesiastical authority, that continued to sing only of its separate God's love for His human creation, and lay authority, that now condemned Amor as being immature, impractical and irrational "puppy love." By the mid-20th century ecclesiastical authority still insisted on adherence to its medieval doctrine while lay authority, reflecting the rational world, seductively beckoned the individual away from the "dimension" of human life "within, beyond, and behind 'the sheath of food.'"

But, unaware of the significance of their song, the 20th century troubadours continued to sing of the mystery of love directed toward "this blossoming earth" that their medieval counterparts recognized "as the true domain of love as it is of life." Because the Amor of the troubadours has nothing to do with sin or with the corruption of humankind or nature, it has nothing to do with redemption and salvation as defined by the ecclesiastical authority, still holding to its doctrine of original sin and still reinforcing the need for its sinful children and "pilgrim people" to atone for the sin that corrupted the nature of the individual. Thus authorized Christian love, Agape, of "the charitable church supper type," though enacted on "this blossoming earth," has its eyes cast toward Heaven instead in atonement to the offended God. Christian Agape is a form of penance that, despite its public nature, remains a private matter involving the offending sinner and his or her offended, separate God. The recipient of the charitable love is of little, or no, consequence. The act of charity atones. Hailed as the ultimate in Christian love, Apape, then, is "indiscriminate," being of the domain of Heaven and not of "this blossoming earth." Furthermore, because it is the love of "society, both lay and ecclesiastical" it is "the corruption ruinous" of the love of the troubadours—pagan, medieval or 20th century—who either, consciously or unconsciously, celebrated "not heaven but this blossoming earth as the true domain of love as it is of life."

Ironically, the Church of Rome, up to the convening of its Second Vatican Council, was both an Agape and an Amor institution. Because its God was identified as a distinct personality separate from the individual, He could be loved as another person, as another individual, with the same devotion and commitment one individual can show another in the domain of "this blossoming earth." Thus the Church's sisters, brothers and priests, with their devotion to this Heavenly individual revealed to earthly individuals through Christ, could love in the manner of the earthly, heretical troubadours, making the atonement love of Agape secondary to the at-one-ment love of Amor. But the Church, with its eyes, ears and heart understandably closed to the love song of the troubadours, failed to recognize its Amor character. As a result, its Second Vatican Council, called to usher the Church into our age of scientific inquiry and discovery, authorized Agape as the ultimate expression of Christian love "having the power to enchant and move the world." With its eyes still cast toward Heaven and its separate God, the Church failed to recognize the at-one-ment nature of its Heaven directed, but earthly expression of, Amor. It failed to recognize the "pagan Celtic Being of beings" and the "dimension" of human life "within, beyond, and behind 'the sheath of food.'" It failed to recognize the "collective" identity of individuals that, when lived, has the power not only to "move" but to transform the world.

By the time the Second Vatican Council concluded, 20 years after the atomic explosion at Hiroshima, we, as Western individuals—physically and psychologically removed from our pre-Christian past and losing faith in our institutional vision based on the premise of "mythic dissociation"—found ourselves abandoned in a seemingly meaningless world. Without any "dimension" of human life "within, beyond, or behind 'the sheath of food,'" we complained—through our music—that we could get "no satisfaction." Essentially, individual existence had not changed, but psychologically separated from nature and the love song of its "singers and harpers of the Fairy Hills," we were left to conclude that there is no more to life than death. In effect, the complaint of the abandoned individual, given rousing expression by The Rolling Stones, echoes that of Sartre who complained that "everything indeed is permitted if God does not exist." Thus the 'Satisfaction' era of rock n' roll, continuing to the present day and seemingly beyond, was born. It supplanted the era of the 20th century troubadours, "the singers and harpers from the Fairy Hills," who sang "of certain heroic individuals, who thus stand as epiphanies of that 'manifest hidden' which moves within us all and is the secret of the harmony of nature."

With the waning of the influence of institutional authority—supported by the premise of "mythic dissociation"—and with the 20th century denigration of Amor to the level of infantile "puppy love," the "era of romanticism that is unable to achieve form at all and so smashes out of disparagement and resentment" failed to recognize the "heroic individuals" associated with the songs of the "singers and harpers of the Fairy Hills." Thus the post-troubadour era of rock n' roll smashed and disparaged "out of resentment" and no longer sang, either by accident or design, of that mysterious power of Amor which is that "manifest hidden" and "which moves and lives within us all and is the secret of the harmony of nature." With the death of God as the Christian West had known Him since the days of St. Augustine, we were left without God. As a result, we could get "no satisfaction" and "smashed and disparaged" in "resentment" of the realization that we had been the victims of a lie. The result in song was neither a celebration of the Amor of the "singers and harpers of the Fairy Hills" nor a celebration of the Agape of the offending institution. Instead, the result was a celebration of Eros which is "natural and fleshly being 'the urge and delight of sex.'"

"The singers and harpers of the Fairy Hills" did not equate love with sex because authentic love, Amor, is born of the eyes and the heart. It is the love of power and majesty that awakens the "'manifest hidden' which moves within us all and is the secret of the harmony of nature." It is the love expressed by the medieval troubadour, Guirant de Bornail, whom Joseph Campbell—in 'Creative Mythology'—identifies as "perhaps the greatest of all." The words from his poem reveal his vision:

> So, through the eyes love attains the heart;
> For the eyes are scouts of the heart,
> And the eyes go reconnoitering;
> For what it would please the heart to possess.
> And when they are in full accord
> And firm all three, in one resolve,
> At that time perfect love is born
> From what the eyes have made welcome to the heart.
> Not otherwise can love either be born or have commencement.
> Than by this birth and commencement moved by inclination.
>
> By the grace and by command
> Of these three, and from their pleasure
> Love is born, who with fair hope
> Goes comforting her friends
> For as all true lovers
> Know, love is the perfect kindness,
> Which is born—there is no doubt—from the heart and eyes.
> The eyes which make it blossom; the heart that matures it:
> Love, which is the fruit of their very seed.

Such love of power and majesty surely isn't "rational" and just as surely isn't "puppy love." Neither is it "indiscriminate" Agape love motivated by penitent atonement, popular guilt or simple convenience. Instead, it is the sacrificial love of at-one-ment. And in an era of the Christian West that has witnessed the death of its "traditional" God, it is the love that is God—that "'manifest hidden' which moves and lives within us all and is the secret of the harmony of nature."

Perhaps the most representative 20th century answers to the "pagan Celtic singers and harpers of the Fairy Hills" and the medieval troubadours are Ricky Nelson, Buddy Holly and Elvis Presley. In songs like 'Hello, Mary Lou,' Peggy Sue,' and 'Don't Be Cruel' each celebrates Amor "whose music has the power to enchant and move the world; to make men weep, to make men sleep, and to make men laugh." The power of Amor allows the individual to "remain as a child," and thus its singers "appear mysteriously from the Land of Eternal Youth," reminding all individuals of that "'manifest hidden'" that lives "within us all and is the secret of the harmony of nature" whose "very heart" is love. Buddy Holly sings of "pretty, pretty Peggy Sue" and "my heart yearns for you" and "I love you girl and I need you, Peggy Sue." Elvis Presley doesn't name the beloved in 'Don't Be Cruel,' but still he sings "don't want no other love, baby it's just you

I'm thinking of" and "don't be cruel to a heart that's true." Both songs and both troubadours—each representative of their era—clearly sing about "what all true lovers know"—"love is perfect kindness which is born—there is no doubt—from the heart and eyes."

In each instance the love is discriminately directed to an individual, and its fulfillment only can be realized in that particular individual. In both instances the love celebrated is neither the "indiscriminate" charity of Agape, where the penitent act is more important than the individual recipient, nor the just as indiscriminate passion of Eros, where the impulse to love is a response to "the urge, desire, and delight of sex." Both songs celebrate the individual's, and not a separate God's, capacity for love—for Amor. They identify the individual human being, then, as the creative force in the world, living as Dr. Jung would say, as "an incarnation and revelation of God himself."

But perhaps no song of the troubadour era of rock n' roll expresses that spirit, and thus the very heart of this musical form, as freshly and as exuberantly as does 'Hello, Mary Lou.' Like Buddy Holly's 'Peggy Sue' Ricky Nelson's song directly and discriminately identifies a specific individual by name as the object of love. But it more emphatically celebrates the troubadour belief, emerging from natural experience, of the link between the eyes, "the noblest sense" uncorrupted by any sin, and the heart. 'Hello Mary Lou,' perhaps more clearly than any other song of rock n' roll's troubadour era, celebrates the individual, naturally evocative experience with love that begins with the eyes—"hello, Mary Lou"—and travels to the heart—"goodbye heart." This natural, evocative experience with love, because it has the power to "enchant and move" an individual, clearly has the power to "enchant and move the world." And as long as we see the world as the sum total of individuals capable of being enchanted and moved, those who respond to the call of Amor are neither abandoned to its meaninglessness nor "condemned to be free." Instead, they live the "dimension" of human life "within, beyond, and behind 'the sheath of food.'" They aren't abandoned or condemned because they are living God as heroic individuals who thus stand as epiphanies of that "'manifest hidden' which moves within us all and is the secret of the harmony of nature."

Thus the lovers celebrated in songs like 'Peggy Sue, 'Don't Be Cruel' and 'Hello, Mary Lou' are individual incarnations and revelations of "God Himself." Prior to the waning of the power and influence of institutional authority, supported by the premise of "mythic dissociation," we had no need to consciously recognize this God because faith in authority's God, though weakening, still was strong. And the structure and order of individual lives, built on that faith, still was intact. However, due to the impact of the evidence associated with accumulated experience and scientific discovery, that faith is weaker—and in many cases non-existent—as the human race enters the 21st century. In his study of 'The Undiscovered Self' Dr. Jung tells us that faith is grounded in experience, and like Mark Twain's Huckleberry Finn we "don't take no stock in dead people." But an individual who experiences Amor in all its anguish and rapture can believe in it as an expression of that "'manifest hidden' which moves within us all and is the secret of the harmony of nature." As individuals, we can experience God right now while we live, and in so doing we can live as incarnations and revelations of "God Himself." This God, celebrated in the music of the pagan minstrels and the medieval and 20th-century troubadours, knows no personality, lives in the "Land below Waves," and when awakened, can emerge in every individual member of the species—both male and female without distinction or discrimination.

And for this God, the God of Experience, to be awakened, we need only live the "true heart" of the lovers celebrated in the representative songs of Buddy Holly, Elvis Presley and Ricky Nelson. The "true heart" is Freidrich Neitzche's "strong spirit" who is "free" to have a "conscience." The "true heart" is obedient to the call of Amor which is not the institutional call of the God—separate from individual human beings—who demands atonement. Instead, it is the individual call of the God—inherent in us all—who commands at-one-ment. When discovered, brought to the level of consciousness and lived, this God of Experience holds the power to "move" and transform the world. It's no wonder, then—especially when seen in the light of 20th-century psychological insight—that the love song of the "singers and harpers of the Fairy Hills" had the power "to make men weep, to make men sleep, and to make men laugh." The love song of those "singers and harpers" had the power to transform any "true heart," or "strong spirit," into a "heroic individual," an "epiphany," a living expression "of that 'manifest hidden' which moves within us all and is the secret of the harmony of nature."

For the medieval poet and champion of Amor, Gottfried von Strassburg, a "true heart" or "strong spirit" was a "noble heart." In 'Creative Mythology' Joseph Campbell refers to Gottfried's "most learned and discerning interpreter," Gottfried Weber, to explain such a heart:

> it opens inward toward the mystery of character, destiny and worth, and at the same time outward, toward the world and the wonder of beauty, where it sets the lover at odds, however, with the moral order.

Thus the lovers celebrated in the songs of the rock n' roll troubadours as "true hearts" opened "inward toward the mystery of character, destiny and worth" found their eyes opened to that "dimension within, beyond, and behind what in India is termed 'the sheath of food,' the tangible, visible forms of phenomenality." Their eyes were opened to what we, now living in an era marked by the waning of the power and influence of institutional authority, can recognize as God—revealed by rock n' roll's troubadour music, however accidentally, from "the Land below Waves."

Also, the lovers celebrated in those songs were set "at odds with the moral order." To obey the call of Amor, they had to live apart from a moral order that termed their devotion "puppy love" and recognized rational marriage as the authentic end—purpose—of a rational life where physical love could gratify the glands, satisfy the "urge" or produce children to help populate God's Kingdom. The lovers celebrated in the songs of the rock n' roll troubadours speak of marriage only after they have experienced Amor that is born in the eyes and the heart. "Let's walk to the preacher and let us say I do," the lover in 'Don't Be Cruel' says to his beloved, elevating marriage to the sacramental status it deserves as having the power to sanctify love that already exists in the eyes and heart. Such a union between two "noble hearts," is indestructible and is the dream—the aspiration—of any "noble heart," "strong spirit" or "true heart." Such a union is a manifestation of the creative power of love that has the capacity to unite a world that is the sum total of individuals in need of unity.

But just as it was for the medieval troubadours, the "moral order," the "public order," was "ruinous to love" for their 20th century counterparts. To obey the call of Amor the "heroic individual," who surfaced in either troubadour era, had to disobey the "moral order," the "public order" of society either "lay" or "ecclesiastical" or both. To obey the sanctioned "order," the individual had to suppress the natural call to Amor and, therefore, had to delay—and perhaps even prevent—the just as natural "incarnation" and "revelation" of the "mystery" of his or her "character, destiny and worth." In short, the Western individual could not walk the Way of the Cross, symbolically expressed through Christianity's crucifix—its eloquent image of the universal "heroic individual," the God that lives within us all as that "'manifest hidden'" and who "is the secret of the harmony of nature."

Like the lovers celebrated in the songs of the 20th century troubadours, Christ, in his crucified image on the cross, is "set at odds with the moral order." He saw "not heaven but this blossoming earth as the true domain of love as it is of life"—"the Kingdom of the Father is spread upon the earth and men do not see." Men did not, and do not, see because the "moral order" enforced by ecclesiastical authority tells them that the Kingdom is elsewhere, that heaven and not "this blossoming earth" is "the true domain of love as it is of life." Certainly, "this blossoming earth" is a "vale of tears" because, as the Buddha says—and as the crucifix reinforces—"all life is sorrowful." Life is supposed to be sorrowful. But with the acceptance and affirmation of that necessity comes the recognition of rapture. And the "heroic individual," celebrated in troubadour songs, or in mythic symbols, directing his or her attention to "this blossoming earth as the true domain of love as it is of life," walks the streets of Ricky Nelson's "Lonesome Town where the broken hearts stay" but is free to experience that rapture in the form of "perfect love" born when the eyes and the heart "are in full accord and firm." The "heroic individual," in quiet disobedience to the established "moral order," lives the "moral order" of Amor which, as we know, is "the path directly before one of the eyes and their message to the heart."

In obedience to nature's call of Amor, therefore, the "heroic individual," as an "epiphany" of that "'manifest hidden' which moves within us all," lives as an expression of "the harmony of nature." Such an individual walks the path of redemption, salvation and immortality, all to be experienced here and now on "this blossoming earth" which was then, is now and always will be "the true domain of love as it is of life." Referring to this realization of the Amor lover, Joseph Campbell thinks that "we have here attained, I would say, new ground." But more accurately, I think we "have attained," instead, a rediscovery of ancient ground already walked by a succession of "noble hearts" who displayed the courage to answer nature's call of Amor, live its "moral order" and experience—in the words of Gottfried von Strassburg—"dear life and sorrowful death, dear death and sorrowful life." The "heroic individual," celebrated in troubadour songs and in our own crucifix, gives concrete expression to Gottfried's own sentiments when he states at the beginning of his Prologue to his story of 'Tristan': "in this world let me have my life, to be damned with it or to be saved."

The "heroic individual" lives forever in the creative illusions of troubadour music—from "the Land below Waves"—and religion, lending support to Joseph Campbell's conviction, revealed in "The Impact of Science on Myth" from 'Myths to Live By,' that "life needs life supporting illusions." Christianity and the songs of the troubadour era of rock n' roll, both belonging to this necessary world, support life by offering the inspiration the "true heart," the "noble heart," the "strong spirit" needs to live beyond the level of "the innocence of Eden" that "prevailed until, at some point in time, the eyes which along the lines of animal life had evolved as agents of the quest for nourishment were opened to a dimension within." At that "point in time in the course of the last 3 1/2 <u>million</u> years" individuals awakened to "awe" with their "awakening to the mystery of death."

With the "awakening to the mystery of death," human beings sought to explain, through "life supporting illusions," the mystery of the transcendence of that reality which, of course, is the mystery of life. Music and religion are part of—as opposed to apart from—the "life supporting" world of mythology. The song of the troubadours, regardless of the era, and the song of the crucifix celebrate obedience to nature's call to Amor as representing the transcendent path that leads to redemption and salvation. Such a life, in turn, guarantees immortality to the "heroic individual" who lives as an "incarnation and revelation of God himself." With our rediscovery of God, we can return, consciously, to those mythological expressions belonging to the order of "the romanticism of true power that shatters contemporary forms to go beyond them to new forms." Then in our "new forms" we can celebrate the Amor spirit of the troubadours—the lost heart of rock n' roll and the still undiscovered heart of Christianity—that, finally, gives clear expression to the essence of us all.

5

The Undiscovered Morality of Amor

To honestly understand the concept of morality, we have to be free to acknowledge the antiquity of our civilization that takes us beyond the boundaries we usually associate with its Christian era. We have to acknowledge that Christianity did not invent morality and that its emergence did not necessarily introduce moral behavior into a morally bankrupt world. If we are free to explore the concept of morality with the proper curiosity and wonder—"as a child"—in obedience to the teachings of Christianity's crucified savior, we are free to discover, without fear of punishment, the morality of the responsible individual—the Morality of Amor.

If we are as free to explore our moral terrain as we have been to explore our earthly and celestial terrain, the word pagan then assumes different connotations. Instead of dismissing it as referring to a time of complete amorality, or at least complete immorality, we can understand it as referring to an historical period of the West, preceding its Christian era, that was marked by living expressions of what constituted moral, immoral and amoral behavior. When we view our civilization in all its antiquity, we can't dismiss the pagan era as being a period of uncivilized immoral behavior made moral by the emergence of Christianity and its institutionally authoritative moral code. Only with properly balanced vision, that sees the West's pagan era as being equivalent to its succeeding Christian era, can we begin to understand ourselves—and our individual identity—as we progress through the 21st century and beyond.

The Morality of Amor is born out of natural experience, and, as we have seen, experientially civilized humanity was born with "the awakening of awe" that occurred "at some unrecorded moment in the course of the last 3 1/2 million years" when, as Joseph Campbell also informs us, the individual human being awakened to "the mystery of death and therewith of life." This awakening, Mr.

Campbell continues, "more than any other physical transformation—elevated man above the level of the beast, 'that (according to culture historian Oswald Spengler) live but know nothing of life, and that die and see death,' as Spengler remarks, 'without knowing anything about it.'" Without interference, no matter how well-intentioned, from any institutional authority, civilized individuals—identified with the "awakening of awe"—had to accept death as a necessary (if not natural) part of life from which no individual was excluded. With this "awakening of awe at some unrecorded moment in the course of the last 31/2 million years," the human soul was born. And the morality of the responsible individual—the Morality of Amor—in turn springs from that soul.

In the Christian era of Western civilization this still undiscovered morality finally emerged in the Middle Ages as "the courtly cult of amor" and found expression in the poetry of the medieval troubadours in whose lyrics "we hear little or nothing of the fall and corruption either of the senses or of the world." The non-experiential authority of the Christian church introduced the Western individual to "the fall" and also to its institutional morality, built on the accompanying premises of original sin and "mythic dissociation." Opposition to this institutional morality emerged, both out of rebellion and out of an authentic quest for truth, in the Middle Ages and oftentimes was met with a trip to the stake—the medieval answer to crucifixion. By the 18th century the awakening of reason had joined the natural accumulation of experience as a threat to the coercive power of institutional Christian morality. And by our 21st century, following voyages to the moon and telescopic exploration into the farthest reaches of the universe, reason and naturally accumulated experience have triumphed, rendering that morality, built on original sin and its complementary premise of "mythic dissociation," obsolete.

The affective demise of traditional, institutional Christian morality is part of the continuing emergence of Western civilization and, ironically, part of the reemergence of the individual now aware of, and able to accept, death as a necessary—and even natural—part of the mystery of life. With the rediscovery of this mystery can come the reawakening of awe and the rediscovery of religion and literature—of mythology—as our experientially inspired expression of what Dr. Eiseley, in 'The Firmament of Time,' terms "the personal ethic of individual, responsible men" that "no group ethic ever could, or should, replace." In the newly rediscovered world of mythology, inclusive of religion and literature covering both our pagan and Christian eras, "the personal ethic of individual, responsible men" is revealed in the Hero who can wear any one of a "thousand faces" and who is a timeless expression of evocative experience rather than an ephemeral creation of well-intentioned coercive authority.

Freed from the visionary constraints of original sin, and therefore free to explore our religion as part of—rather than apart from—the more universal world of mythology, we can discover the "personal ethic of individual, responsible men."

For example, the crucified Hero of the Christian Mythology does not surrender his individual soul, and therefore does not relinquish control over his own life, to a "group ethic" that doesn't consciously or unconsciously reinforce the awakened "personal ethic" of a responsible individual. In this instance the "personal ethic" of the responsible individual comes into conflict with the "group ethic" of the institutional structure. The "personal ethic" of the responsible individual—revealed through the "face" of Christ—acknowledges, for example, the unity of the individual and the Father ("I and my Father are one") whereas the "group ethic" of the institutional structure proclaims the separation of the two. In addition, while the "personal ethic," revealed through the "face" of Christ, is built on a premise of "mythic association," the "group ethic," in this case revealed through the Old Testament, Pharisaic authority, is built on a premise of "mythic dissociation."

Furthermore, when we view it with eyes freed from the visionary constraints of original sin, the "group ethic" of the New Testament Christian authority is built on the "mythic dissociation" premise as well and therefore regards the "personal ethic"—as did the Old Testament, Pharisaic authority—as being blasphemous or heretical. In effect, we saw little, fundamental change in the supposed transition from the Old Testament Law to the New Testament Law. Because it is built on the institutionally authorized premise of "mythic dissociation," rather than on the experientially inspired premise of "mythic association," the New Testament Law is not actually new. The resulting institutional church, then, holding fast to its doctrine of original sin, remains as much an impediment to individual maturation as was its Old Testament, Pharisaic predecessor. As a result, the contemporary responsible individual is faced with the same conflict illuminated by the Christian symbol of the crucifix. Such an individual is faced with the fact that the emerging "personal ethic," revealed in the crucified Christ, conflicts with the "group ethic" of the institutional structure now represented by the Christian authority of the New Testament, replacing the Pharisaic authority of the Old Testament.

The "personal ethic," regardless of when or where it emerges, acknowledges the union of humanity and God and thus is built on the premise of "mythic association" rather than on the opposing premise of "mythic dissociation." The resulting, inevitable conflict between a responsible individual and institutional authority, what Faulkner might call "the human heart in conflict with itself," is constant throughout the experiential, mythological history of the Christian West. In that history any natural movement toward individual maturation is impeded by the presence of the Christian authority as a Western expression of a Middle Eastern idea supposedly laid to rest as an example of "the shells of forms produced and left behind by lives once lived." Such an idea supposedly was laid to rest by the sacrificial life of the World Savior in the "face" of Christ, crucified—alienated—because of his obedience to the "personal ethic of individual, responsible men" that "no group ethic ever could, or should, replace." The sacrificial life of the Hero, revealed through the "face" of Christ and preserved forever by the New Testament Christian Mythology, predates—by almost 2,000 years—Jung's reasonable, experiential conclusion that tells us "we cannot live the afternoon of life according to the program of life's morning." We have to remember that "what was great in the morning will be little at evening, and what in the morning was true will at evening have become a lie."

Had the desert Middle East's Pharisaic authority been as responsible as the crucified, individual Hero of the Christian Mythology, it would have discovered—in its Garden of Eden story—support for the Hero's seemingly blasphemous claims. Freed from the restraints of institutional interpretation, the Garden of Eden story presents Adam and Eve as responsible individuals—although Adam is more reluctant than Eve—faced with the same dilemma where their emerging "personal ethic," expressed through the serpent, surfaces in conflict with the "group ethic," this time expressed through God, or Yahweh as the Old Testament expression of God. Mirroring the same conflict identified in the story of Christ and his opposing Pharisaic authority, Adam and Eve's dilemma essentially reflects a conflict of obedience—thus "the human heart in conflict with itself." And obedience is one of the dominant virtues of the responsible individual open to the emergence of the morality of the "personal ethic," the Morality of Amor. When we look with the curious and wondering eyes of "a child," Adam and Eve—by eating the apple in disobedience of God but in obedience to the serpent—follow "the way of the heart," or the Way of the Cross for their successor, Christ. A responsible authority—a serpent authority—illuminates this "way" in support of the individual, thereby making the walking of that path less painful and less alienating. But the "group ethic"—whether expressed through Eden's desert God, the institutional Pharisaic authority or the institutional Christian authority—never has supported the individual's quest for fulfillment or "individuation." Thus the individual's passage through "the stages of life" toward that end has been more difficult than it should be.

The responsible individual, revealed here in the "faces" of Adam and Eve and Christ, obeys the Serpent authority—"the personal ethic of responsible, individual men." That authority lives in our unconscious identity and could be reinforced and awakened by the institutional authority, if it were to play the role experience assigns to the Serpent of Eden and not that which authority assigns to the God of Eden. Ironically, the undiscovered God of the Old Testament—and the God of the Morality of Amor—is the Serpent who appears again, this time fully mature and realized in Christ, as the New Testament expression of God. Reinforcing Christ as the New Testament expression of God promotes, as well as authorizes, the living of the noble and honorable "personal ethic of individual, responsible men" as "the way of the heart," the Way of the Cross, the way of salvation and redemption.

In his story of Huckleberry Finn's adventures, Mark Twain makes it clear that the New Testament authority did not promote this "way of the heart" as being the way of salvation and redemption. Following the Civil War, America was in need of redemption but not of the kind associated with the New Testament authority proclaiming its doctrine of original sin. Instead, America was in need of enlightenment—of maturation. The country was in need of the redemption associated with the awakening of the "personal ethic of individual, responsible men" that only can emerge in a psychological environment not charged with original sin. Therefore, the Christian authority, expressed through the character of Miss Watson in Twain's story, is not redeemed because it is not enlightened. First of all, a redeemed, mature authority does not condone, and even authorize, slavery. Furthermore, and even more importantly, such an authority does not suggest—to a responsible individual more interested in what is right and true than he is in what is comfortable and convenient—that the way to salvation and redemption runs contrary to the path of the emerging "way of the heart." Acting contrary to responsible Serpent authority, but in accord with its doctrine of original sin, the New Testament Christian authority of 19th century America tells Huck, the responsible individual wearing a unique, American "face," that the right and true path demands that he reveal the secret whereabouts of Jim, Miss Watson's runaway slave and his companion in adventure.

In his responsible commitment to do what is right and true, Huck, a child of the river—of nature reminiscent of our pagan, pre-Christian past—initially decides to write Miss Watson a note revealing Jim's hiding place. But, finally, he decides to tear up his note of obedience to the irresponsible dictates of the New Testament authority:

> It was a close place. I took it up, and held it in my hand. I was a-trembling because I'd got to decide, forever, betwixt two things, and I knowed it. I studied a minute, sort of holding my breath, and then says to myself: 'All right, then, I'll go to Hell'—and tore it up.

Huckleberry Finn, as an expression of the responsible individual awakened to the "mystery of life," has to "challenge Hell," in the manner of the medieval Hero in the Grail romance, in order to follow "the way of the heart." But a responsible, Serpent authority, freed from—or ignorant of—original sin would have illuminated that "way," the Way of the Cross, thereby facilitating Huck's—the responsible individual's—path to "individuation."

Huck's responsible decision to obey "the way of the heart," or the "personal ethic," in opposition to the way of irresponsible authority, or the "group ethic," is "forever" and he "knowed it." Huck's contemporary counterparts, when faced with a similar expression of the same conflict, know the decision is "forever" as well, as long as the authority in question continues to illuminate the path of irresponsibility—the "group ethic"—in opposition to the path of responsibility—the "personal ethic of individual, responsible men." Due to the impact of the discoveries of rational science and the results of our extensive, experiential exploration of our celestial terrain, Huck's contemporary counterparts no longer have to "challenge Hell." But any responsible individual does have to endure the alienation revealed through Huck who reckoned he "got to light out for the territory ahead of the rest because Aunt Sally she's going to adopt and sivilize me, and I can't stand it. I been there before."

Ironically, the irresponsible authority that would "sivilize" Huck is uncivilized itself. The way of the responsible individual, the way of the "personal ethic," the "way of the heart," the Way of the Cross is the proper way of civilization. For authority to be civilized and for it to further the cause of "individuation" and civilization, it has to illuminate, in the manner of the Serpent of Eden, this "way of the heart" that Huck has to "challenge" authority's Hell to follow. If given the opportunity to live the Morality of Amor by established, institutional authority whom we have historically obeyed, any of us choosing to avoid that "way" would be held responsible for our own tragic demise. But as Geoffrey Chaucer asked in the prologue to his 13th century 'Canterbury Tales': "if the gold rusts, what shall the iron do?" In the heroic spirit of the responsible individual correcting authority "holding to the shells of forms produced and left behind by lives once lived," the "iron" can decide—in the name of redemption and salvation—to search for, to discover and then to live the "personal ethic of responsible, individual men." The "iron" can decide to search for, to discover and then to live the "way of the heart."

Certainly, the discovery of the Morality of Amor is made easier if established authority, regardless of its "face," does not "rust." However, the Old Testament Pharisaic authority had rusted as had the New Testament Christian authority, creating a situation where responsible individuals, on their journey to "individuation," had to disobey that authority and endure the pain of alienation in order to achieve and live their destiny. Ideally, the established authority should play the role a curious reading of the Garden of Eden story assigns to the serpent, thus illuminating the path of "individuation," the path of destiny, for responsible individuals now free to make their own decisions. The tribal, parental or institutional authority should seek to awaken the individual's natural sense of responsibility. Ideally, the responsible Serpent authority should seek to awaken, by accident or design, the individual's unconscious identity that Dr. Jung concluded to be "collective." And ironically, we find that a pagan warrior chief, Hrothgar, from the pre-Christian, Anglo-Saxon epic 'Beowulf,' plays that very role of the redeemed, enlightened authority. Furthermore, he does so without ever having heard of the Christian serpent or the Christian Yahweh, whether gleaned from a curious or closed reading of the Garden of Eden story.

Bewoulf, the epic Hero who lends his name to the story, is a responsible individual wearing the "face" of a pagan warrior. Given his sense of loyalty, obedience and commitment to what is right and true more than to what is comfortable and convenient, he is equivalent to any other responsible individual—pagan or Christian—wearing any other "face." He is equivalent to any other Hero wearing any one of a "thousand faces." When we read it with freedom and the appropriate curiosity, Beowulf's story of psychological maturation is equivalent to Christ's and Huckleberry Finn's. The pagan warrior "face" may differ from the "faces" associated with Christ and Huck, but the three individuals—beneath their radically different "faces"—are distinguished by their sense of responsibility and by their subsequent identity with the "personal ethic," with the Morality of Amor. All three, spanning the pagan and Christian era of Western civilization, are equivalent expressions of "individuation" and thus of the individual's "collective," unconscious identity. And all three encounter authority on their road to psychological transformation and maturation, their road to "individuation." But only Beowulf encounters an authority who seeks to release, rather than suppress, his unconscious identity. Only the pagan expression of a responsible, Heroic individual encounters an authentic Serpent authority who illuminates the sacrificial demands of the Morality of Amor.

Beowulf, the warrior Geat loyal to his King Hygelac, is drawn to Hrothgar's Danish kingdom—ravaged by the monster, Grendel—by the promise of fame that he will win if he can put an end to the monster's terrorizing, nightly escapades. Eventually, he defeats both Grendel and his vengeful mother, winning glory and honor for himself and for his king and, at the same time, distinguishing himself to be a man with the power, determination and courage to back up his mighty boasts. But Beowulf's boastful arrogance did not convince Hrothgar to allow him into his kingdom in the first place. Being "old of winters," Hrothgar's experienced eyes recognized Beowulf's potential for humility—his potential to live as a responsible individual. Having lived in obedience to the naturally emerging "personal ethic" himself, Hrothgar has earned the right to "preach" to Beowulf, and he chooses the appropriate moment when Beowulf stands at the height of his fame and glory—the moment when the warrior Hero is most susceptible to pride.

Hrothgar does speak of "how in His great spirit mighty God gives wisdom to mankind" and of how "He possesses power over all things," but in spite of the imposition of orthodox Christian imagery, 'Beowulf' remains a pagan epic that pre-dates the coming of Christianity—with its separate God—to Western Europe. Hrothgar, then, primarily is a pagan warrior chief whose wisdom derives not from the dictates of institutional authority but from the inspiration of natural experience. Therefore, as a tribal, Serpent authority his teaching reinforces—rather than refutes—Beowulf's emerging "personal ethic." In effect, Hrothgar is an expression of the infallibility authority enjoys when it reinforces the wisdom of considered, accumulated experience. He is not infallible simply by virtue of his authoritative status. As a reflection of his infallibility and in expression of the pagan warrior virtues of obedience and respect for age, "all were silent" when the noble king spoke.

"Lo, this may one say who works truth and right for the folk, recalls all things distant, an old guardian of the land: that this earl was born the better man." Hrothgar has earned the right to speak because he has worked "truth and right for the folk." He is a responsible individual more interested in what is right and true than he is in what is comfortable and convenient. He rules "for the folk" out of love and humility. Moreover, he "recalls all things far distant" and not only those "things" that support institutional dogma and doctrine. He is "an old guardian of the land" and a noble, responsible individual devoted to "the folk" and to the performance of his duty, even if such devotion proves to be uncomfortable and inconvenient. He is an authentic Hero with the "affect power" to touch Gottfried von Strassburg's "noble heart." Beowulf is such a "noble heart," and having ascended to the height of his fame and glory, he stands among those who listen in silent reverence and respect to the wisdom of the grizzled warrior king.

Hrothgar, the Serpent authority, tells Beowulf that "all of it, all of your strength, you govern steadily in the wisdom of your heart." He tells Beowulf to govern in accord with "the way of the heart," the way of love, the way of Amor. And he tells him that he "shall become a comfort, whole and long lasting to your people, a help to warriors." Hrothgar tells Beowulf that he will govern in humility, that he will place his emerging sense of duty above any rewards associated with this most respected of roles in the warrior society. The experienced warrior king is aware of the dangers of pride that increase in direct proportion to the prestige of the social role and its accompanying rewards. Hrothgar knows, then, that Beowulf is more susceptible to pride than is someone who, for whatever reason, is denied access to a social role as attractive and as prestigious as that which he is destined to live. When we, as Western individuals, explore our moral terrain with the courage and wonder we displayed in exploring our earthly and celestial terrain, we discover that Hrothgar's pagan wisdom is another expression of Christ's Christian wisdom when that Hero speaks of it being easier for a camel to pass through the eye of a needle than it is for a rich man to enter the Kingdom of Heaven. Like Hrothgar, Christ speaks from the wisdom of experience out of a sense of "truth and right," and, as a responsible individual, he seeks not to abolish authority but to correct it instead. He builds his New Testament on eternal principles that are neither pagan nor Christian exclusively.

Hrothgar knows that Beowulf, who already has grown great, will grow greater still. Realizing that this greatness can awaken our universal capacity for pride, that lives within Beowulf as an aspect of his unconscious identity, Hrothgar tells the story of Heremod, a warrior-King who was not a "comfort" to "the sons of Ecwela, the Honor-Scyldings." He "grew great not for their joy, but for their slaughter, for the destruction of the Danish people. With swollen heart he killed his table companions." In effect, Heremod governed out of pride and not out of humility. He governed more out of a quest for pleasure and power that he did out of a sense of commitment and love. Beowulf, clearly in control of his own destiny, can freely choose to rule in the manner of Heremod for the "slaughter" of his "folk" or he can rule in the manner of Hrothgar for their "comfort." He is presented with a clear choice between living his capacity for pride, sealing his and his peoples' destruction, and living his capacity for humility, sealing his and his peoples' salvation. Heremod, who chose the path of pride, gave "no rings to the Danes for glory" and "lived joyless to suffer pain of that strife, the long-lasting harm of the people" in a manner similar to Shakespeare's Macbeth for whom life, finally, "is a tale told by an idiot full of sound and fury signifying nothing."

Hrothgar, the Serpent authority, tells Beowulf to "be mindful of munificence" and "to keep yourself against that wickedness, beloved Beowulf, best of men, and choose better—eternal gains. Have no care for pride, great warrior." And Hrothgar, without the slightest mention of original sin in the Garden of Eden, tells Beowulf honestly that:

> for a time there is glory in your might: yet soon it shall be that sickness or sword will diminish your strength, or fire's fangs, or flood's surge, or sword's swing, or spear's flight, or appalling age; brightness of eyes will fail and grow dark; then it shall be that death will overcome you, warrior.

Experientially awakened to "the mystery of death and therewith of life," Hrothgar knows that death is a necessary part of life. Awakened to awe in the face of this mystery, he, as the Serpent authority neither Christ nor Huckleberry Finn encountered, illuminates for Beowulf "the way of the heart"—the way of Amor—and ultimately the way of salvation, redemption and immortality in transcendence of death. Hrothgar illuminates for Beowulf the way of humility—the way of the Serpent of Eden—as opposed to the way of pride—the way of the God of Eden. When we are allowed to read it freely with "honest" eyes, the Eden story tells of the pride of "God" who, in contrast to the Serpent and the "personal ethic," emerges as an expression of the morally inferior "group ethic." As did Christ and Huckleberry Finn after them, Adam and Eve chose to obey "the way of the heart," the way of Amor, the way of the Serpent—the way of the authentic God of Eden.

Beowulf escapes the conflict Adam and Eve, Christ and Huckleberry Finn experienced because of his contact with a Serpent authority in the person of Hrothgar. Thus his ascendance to the maturational level reflected in the Morality of Amor is made easier. To ascend to that level Beowulf only has to obey the warrior authority whose wisdom, ideally, is based on experiential premises. But Beowulf can see for himself that Hrothgar is telling "truth and right." In his case authority reinforces experience, giving him a clear choice of either obeying or disobeying the illuminated "way of the heart." If he disobeys this "heart," in the manner of Heremod, he chooses to be alienated from the "group ethic" that ironically, in this expression of pagan morality, is built on the morally superior "personal ethic," the "way of the heart"—the way of Amor. Thus Beowulf's pagan morality, built on the "personal ethic" proves to be superior to Christian morality, built on the "group ethic," because Adam and Eve, Christ and Huckleberry Finn have to disobey Old and New Testament Christian morality to even discover the "personal ethic"—the Morality of Amor. This undiscovered morality, whether given pagan or Christian expression, is the path of creation and not the path of destruction. It is the path of survival, salvation and redemption for the contemporary, Western individual. The path of the Morality of Amor, illuminated for all to see in the Hero wearing any one of a "thousand faces," is the path of "individuation"—the path of the "undiscovered self" for Dr. Jung.

Unlike Heremod, Beowulf chooses to obey "the way of the heart." In so doing he brings order and harmony to his kingdom for 50 years. Once we're free from the visionary constraints of original sin, we can see that to obey the evocative dictates of experience, in disobedience to the coercive dictates of institutional authority, is not to live the sin of pride. On the contrary, to disobey the dictates of institutional authority in order to obey those of experience is to "be mindful of munificence," to guard "against that wickedness" and to "choose better—eternal gains." The Way of the Cross, illuminated by the crucified Hero of the Christian Mythology, is "the way of the heart" that Hrothgar illuminates for Beowulf. Adam and Eve originally illuminated that way in the Garden of Eden and Huckleberry Finn followed suit, once again, in Mark Twain's story of his adventures. Ironically, the Western individual, living under the influence of original sin Christianity, has to disobey the very institutional authority that should "work truth and right for the folk"—the "iron" for whom the "gold" should not "rust"—to ascend to the maturational level, that of the adult ego, associated with the Morality of Amor.

The mythological history of Western civilization, both pagan and Christian, shows that the "personal ethic"—the "way of the heart"—is morally superior to any "group ethic" that isn't built on the humility and compassion of the Amor lover—the Serpent authority. And mythology, in the words of Dr. Jung, proves to be "more individual" and "expresses life more precisely than does science." Furthermore, when we read it scientifically, as an expression of individual psychological potential, rather than historically, as an expression of actual events in historical time, mythology "precisely" reveals the previously undiscovered Morality of Amor that celebrates the individual human being as both the destructive and creative force in the universe The Hero, pagan or Christian, wearing any one of a "thousand faces," is the concrete expression—the incarnation—of this morality which proves to be accessible to all, male and female without distinction or discrimination. Finally, it is a morality made even more accessible when it is reinforced by a responsible Serpent authority "mindful of munificence" and mindful of its responsibility to the "folk"—the iron for whom it, as "gold," should not rust.

When we are as free to explore our moral terrain as we have been to explore our earthly and celestial terrain, we discover—in the words attributed to Christ—that to be "wise as serpents" is to be "harmless as doves." We discover that living the wisdom of the Serpent contributes to the creation of life rather than to its destruction. Also, in the wisdom of the Serpent we discover the Morality of Amor—the "personal ethic of individual, responsible men" that "no group ethic ever could, or should, replace." In the Morality of Amor we rediscover the God of "mythic association" who is a timeless inspiration of evocative experience rather than an ephemeral creation of coercive—no matter how well-meaning—institutional authority. Finally, in the Morality of Amor we discover our capacity, and our responsibility, to live "the personal ethic of individual, responsible men." We learn how each of us can live as a Christ, as a Hero. Each of us discovers the capacity, and the responsibility, to live as "an incarnation and revelation of God himself" in quiet, but majestic, correction of authority "holding to the shells of forms produced and left behind by lives once lived."

6

From the Cathedral to the Shopping Mall

The cathedral served as the structuring symbol of life in medieval Europe, and it still stands, in all its architectural grandeur, in tribute to the majesty that was. By the 16th century the monsters had obscured the majesty sufficiently to warrant reform of the Church, resulting in the Protestant Reformation. That movement subsequently swelled into a multitude of Protestant churches, leaving Western civilization in spiritual disarray as the counter-reformed Roman Catholic Church and its various challengers each claimed to be Christ's Church. Nonetheless, the cathedral, now in both its Roman Catholic and Protestant expressions, continued to serve as the focal point for European life. And as the boundaries of Western civilization extended further westward, that structure played the same role in American life. The cathedral, whether variously Protestant or singularly Roman Catholic, served Western civilization—and its American expression—well into the 20th century of its Christian era. But the post-World War II Western world, led by America, witnessed unparalleled economic progress, and by the mid-1950s the American heartland had given birth to the competing symbol of economic salvation—the shopping mall.

The development of the shopping mall, with the first, modern covered mall reportedly opening in Enid, Minnesota, on October 7, 1956, was inevitable. And given our vast open spaces that easily can accommodate suburban expansion, accompanied by our impatient commitment to economic growth, its development in America was just as predictable. Post-World War II suburban expansion guaranteed the emergence of the air-conditioned, covered shopping mall that could offer its patrons convenient protection from the natural elements that haunt the American landscape and hinder the American shopper. Also, the emergence of the shopping mall coincided with the birth of the Nuclear Age and the era of space exploration that would take us—all of us through the miracle of television—beyond the clouds and beyond the boundaries of earth's atmosphere into the heavens where the Heaven of the cathedral doctrine was supposed to be.

Fueled by the American spirit of adventure, the Western individual's questing nature experientially tested, for the first time, the cherished cathedral doctrine that spoke of a Heavenly Kingdom of God as being separate from the earthly Kingdom of His Creations. If we were to find experiential evidence of the existence of such a Kingdom, celestial exploration would reinforce cathedral doctrine, lending it scientific credibility. Then we could take comfort in the fact that our earthly life, if we lived in accord with the cathedral's laws, would lead to eternal life in union with God in Heaven. In short, any discovery of experiential evidence reinforcing the existence of this Heavenly Kingdom would enhance the credibility of the noble—or mythological—dimension to earthly existence, granting believing individuals a status beyond that of T. S. Eliot's "hollow men" or "men of straw." Such believers, their faith in the mythological promise of life strengthened by their own scientific discoveries, easily could have resisted the call of the more immediate—as well as the more comfortable and convenient—economic promise of the shopping mall.

But by the end of the 1960s, culminating with our triumphant walk on the surface of the moon, the journeys of the courageous, 20th-century celestial explorers had produced no such evidence. Furthermore, actual—not imagined—television pictures from the moon's surface revealed a landscape and an environment hostile to anything resembling any experienced earthly existence.

For the 19th-century pioneer the grass was greener in Oregon's Willamette Valley than it was on the Missouri plains. But for the 20th-century individual, having populated earth's Willamette Valleys but still imbued with the pioneer spirit, there was no grass—only dust—covering the lunar surface. We were left with what we had and seemingly with no place else to go. In addition, we lacked any experiential evidence that could support the existence of a Heavenly Kingdom to which we could look for comfort and release.

The scientific triumphs of the 20th century, whether mythologically or rationally inspired, simply have confirmed that "suspicion that was already dawning in the Middle Ages." They have confirmed the "suspicion that the biblical myth of Creation, Fall, and Redemption is historically untrue." But in testifying to its failed historicity, that "suspicion" does not proclaim the "biblical myth" to be completely false. By turning its attention to creating the Kingdom of God on earth—a socio-economic Kingdom built on a foundation of indiscriminate Agape love, the cathedral has answered the scientific triumphs of the past century. However, in the process it still holds to its doctrine of original sin that reinforces its fundamental premise of "mythic dissociation." Thus its promise cannot compete, affectively, with that offered by the glitter of the shopping mall. In light of the cathedral's continued reluctance to acknowledge the confirmation of contemporary science, the individual is left to discover "the final abode of goodness" that Dr. Eiseley declares the "human heart" to be.

Throughout the history of our Christian era we have been instructed to trust the cathedral as that "final abode of goodness." But the discoveries of rational science have shown that trusted authority can lie, if not, automatically, out of malevolence certainly, conclusively, out of ignorance, fear or pride. In answer to the cathedral lie, we have the shopping mall which, in its glorification of immediate, economic concerns, hardly qualifies as the "final abode of goodness." In addition, governments—whether capitalist or communist—can lie. In the manner of the cathedral, they are run by individual human beings who, given our universal susceptibility to the seductive lure of pleasure and power, can be less interested in goodness and truth than they are in securing that power and preserving the resultant pleasure. An honest evaluation of accumulated experience reveals that if the "human heart" isn't the "final abode of goodness," there simply is no such "abode" to be trusted. And individuals ignorant of the "human heart" are left to live in slavery to existential despair and its immediate, shopping mall promise.

But we are not destined to live in such slavery. Instead, we are destined to live in freedom, and Western Christianity celebrates this destiny, in all its majesty, in the crucifix—the New Testament expression of God. The discoveries of rational science have laid the expression of the Old Testament God to rest. This God, wearing either His traditional ogre, or His more contemporary accommodating, "mask," remains separate from—and superior to—the individual, thereby contributing to current feelings of existential despair. But with God unmasked as a result of the triumphs of scientific discovery, we now can see the true God and discover, in the process, the "goodness" of our own individual hearts. We can set ourselves free from any coercive force that, for whatever reason, may still hold us within its grasp.

In reference to the psychological, or mythological, realm of our existence, the "heart" is synonymous with the unconscious. If the cathedral authority, both before and after the triumphs of rational science, acknowledges this unconscious identity, it ultimately accepts it as being essentially sinful. Therefore, we need the cathedral as the vehicle for our salvation. The crucifix, if recognized at all, is associated with that sinful nature, and we satisfy our need for redemption by receiving the grace we earn through our membership in Christ's Church. In this vision the crucifix justifies the presence of the cathedral authority, whose very existence is endangered if its doctrine of redemption is threatened.

However, the cathedral's insistence on our essential sinful nature depends on its "biblical myth" being historically true, a contention no longer tenable in light of the discoveries of rational science and the results of continuing celestial exploration. That "biblical myth" either is false or true in some way as yet unknown to the cathedral authority or to individuals who historically have obeyed it. If that "myth" is in fact false, it should be replaced by science—following Freud's idea—or by the shopping mall and its supporting economic system. In that case life would be without any noble purpose or significance and would have no need for myth. But if the "biblical myth" is in fact true in some still undiscovered way, we would find the noble purpose of an individual life expressed within it.

Because we can't deny the existence of the world of story, it's hard to deny the existence of the unconscious in some way. Regardless of anyone's attitude toward it, we created the story world—inclusive of mythology and religion—and it has to emanate from some source. Individual human beings do possess some creative power of force and depth. To hold that the world of story, or mythology, is "symptomatic of repressions of infantile incest wishes" and to further hold that "all the arts, and particularly religious arts, are similarly pathological; likewise all philosophies"—as Joseph Campbell tells us Freud thought—is dangerous in light of the lack of any visible, unifying force at work in our contemporary world. It's time to at least consider the possibility that the very "arts and particularly religious arts" that Freud declared "pathological" hold the secret to discovering that necessary, unifying force. It's time to at least consider the possibility that we can find, within that world, various expressions of the "human heart as the final abode of goodness." If those "religious arts"—the world of mythology—don't harbor such expressions, we could be witnessing the very end of man that William Faulkner declined "to accept" in his Nobel Prize Address of 1950.

For whatever reason or reasons, Freud—as he indicated in his declaration—equated original sin Christianity, and its historically true "biblical myth," with the extent of religion for the Western individual. Thus he wasn't free to view that mythology with the curiosity and wonder that would have enabled him to recognize the goodness of the "human heart" symbolically expressed in its crucified Hero. Carl Jung, on the other hand and for whatever reason, didn't equate original sin Christianity with religion. As a result, he was free to view its "biblical myth" with the curiosity Freud couldn't muster and was able to discover, within it, the "goodness of the human heart."

In opposition to his mentor, Jung found, using Joseph Campbell as my source once again, that "the imageries of mythology and religion serve positive, life furthering ends." Among other things, this Jungian thought represents a return to the pre-Christian past of Western civilization in which individuals—acting in response to the experienced "monstrous nature of life" and not in reaction to the coercive influence of any cathedral authority—created mythology for the very reason Jung scientifically rediscovered. Living without the glittering promise of the shopping mall and without the political promise of rational government, our predecessors had to do something to give purpose to their existence that took them beyond "what in India is termed, 'the sheath of food.'" If there is no purpose to life beyond that extent, then there is no more to life than death, and we—in our despair—can live for the glittering promise reflected in the shopping mall or for the rational promise expressed in our political systems. However, "the scientific rediscovery of ancient wisdom," to use Dr. Jung's own words in reference to the role of mythology, can lead us out of our "Waste Land" of "hollow men" and "men of straw."

Because our exploration of the celestial terrain has failed to produce any experiential evidence to support the existence of a Heavenly Kingdom presided over by a God separate from us, we can safely conclude that we have no evidence to support the existence of the subterranean Kingdom of Hell either. Once again, contemporary scientific exploration and discovery only has confirmed that the "biblical myth" of Christianity is historically and physically "untrue." It has not proven that "myth" to be false. In confirming the "suspicion" that already had dawned on the medieval mind, our extensive exploration and subsequent discoveries have liberated us from the authoritative restraints associated with the original sin reading of our "biblical myth." We are now free to read it as something that is supposed to serve "positive, life furthering ends." We are free to read it as our expression of the "ancient wisdom" Jung scientifically rediscovered.

Now that the visionary constraints imposed on us by the cathedral doctrine of original sin have been lifted, we are free to discover "the human heart as the final abode of goodness"—especially in light of the fact that no institutional structure of our Christian era has proven to be worthy of that designation. Historically instructed to trust institutional thought, we have experienced the loss of innocence and have plunged into the darkness that we have mistaken to be permanent. In effect, we have followed the Sartrean existentialists who lament the fact that "everything indeed is permitted if God does not exist" and who "cannot discover in the nature either of man or of the universe any sign of inherent order." Those existentialists haven't discovered the "nature of man" because they haven't discovered mythology—and their own Christian Mythology—as an expression of that nature. To such thinkers our newly-won freedom from the influence of coercive authority represents an inevitable step toward our alienated "doom" rather than a necessary step toward our fulfilled destiny.

Whereas the cathedral authority, holding fast to its doctrine of original sin, sees the unconscious as being essentially sin, the experiential, scientific reading of our "biblical myth" leads to the opposite conclusion. Such a reading leads to the conclusion that the unconscious essentially is love that then, repeatedly, is made incarnate in the Hero. Following this reading of the "biblical myth" of Christianity that seeks to discover its "positive, life furthering ends"—in acceptance of the still "monstrous nature of life"—Christ is cast in the role of Hero. As the Hero wearing one of a "thousand faces," Christ is a symbolic expression of "the human heart," a symbolic expression of the "nature of man" and thus a symbolic expression of the "order" inherent in nature. Also, Christ as Hero is equivalent to all, and superior to none, of the other expressions of the same Hero and of the same universal "nature of man." That "nature" remains the undiscovered "inherent order" the adherents to the promise of the shopping mall, or to that of rational politics, never have found. Therefore, they agree, at least tacitly, with Sartre's rational conclusion concerning the nature of God's existence. But a curious study of Christ as Hero, following Jung's thought that says "mythology and religion serve positive, life furthering ends," can answer these Sartrean adherents and can point the way out of our existential darkness—the way out of our "Waste Land" populated by "hollow men" and "men of straw."

Such a study reveals that we have to embrace the virtue of obedience to live the love made incarnate—made Flesh—in the Hero regardless of any individual, identifying "face." Because Christ, as an expression of the individual as Hero, embraces that virtue, he experiences conflict with his established cathedral authority that doesn't reinforce the emerging "heart" of the responsible individual awakened to the mythological dimension of life. If that established authority, the Pharisaic authority in the case of Christ, reinforces that emerging "heart," the individual doesn't experience any conflict. By obeying that authority, then, the individual would be, in fact, obeying the "heart." However, if the established authority doesn't reinforce the emerging "heart" of the responsible individual, a conflict of obedience ensues where the individual has to choose between the established cathedral authority and the "heart." The path of obedience to the supposed guardian of the mythological dimension of life may be more comfortable, but that path does not represent the Way of the Cross. It does not follow the path of the Hero.

If we were not universally susceptible to pride, the cathedral could be—and no doubt would be—the "final abode of goodness" in which we could place unquestioning faith. But we were then, are now and always will be so susceptible—a contention reinforced by both 'Beowulf' and the New Testament story of Christ. In the pagan epic Hrothgar warns Beowulf to "always swallow pride" and to avoid the "swollen heart." Likewise, in the New Testament story of Christ, the Hero—wearing the "face" of the World Teacher—warns that it is "easier for a camel to pass through the eye of a needle than it is for a rich man to enter the Kingdom of Heaven." According to this experiential wisdom, such a Kingdom only opens its gates to those who "swallow" pride and therefore avoid the "swollen heart." In past eras, not marked by scientific discoveries and celestial exploration, the crucifix could live in support of a mythology of sin. Then individuals could see the cathedral as "the final abode of goodness." However, in light of those discoveries and that exploration—that renders the crucifix powerless in support of an obsolete reading of the Christian "biblical myth"—we no longer can place that same faith in the cathedral. With its claims discredited, we can turn—in our subsequent existential despair—to the shopping mall or to rational politics in our search for the "final abode of goodness." We can even retreat into the supposed safety of the cathedral. But none of those scenarios represent progress made toward discovering the essential "goodness" of the "human heart."

Jungian thought, expressed in the inclusive world of mythology, primarily constitutes an experiential psychology of love where the Hero lives as an expression of the Word Made Flesh. Stripped of its experiential, mythological foundation, however, it is deprived of its majesty and is no match for the more rational Freudian perspective. But supported by the affect power of the Christian crucifix, in turn supporting a mythology that celebrates the individual's capacity to create, Jung's inspiring thought springs to life and illuminates the way out of the "Waste Land" inhabited by "hollow men" and "men of straw." The Hero is the Word Made Flesh, and that word is Love. But that Love is not Agape. If the Love made Flesh were Agape, the indiscriminate love identified with the cathedral authority, we would see no alienation of the kind expressed through the crucifixion of Christianity's Hero. The crucifix, instead of being a symbolic expression of redemption from sin, is—more accurately—a symbolic expression of the alienation of the Heroic individual. As a symbolic expression of redemption from sin, the crucifix is—at best—a provincial symbol and—at worst—a dead symbol still seen as supporting the discredited cathedral doctrines of original sin and "mythic dissociation." But as a symbol of the universal alienation of the Heroic individual, the crucifix is a "primordial symbol" that lives in support of a mythology of love. If that love were Agape, the Hero would not be alienated for illuminating the Way of the Cross. Ironically, the Hero is crucified—alienated—simply because he loves in obedience to his "heart" that has experientially proven to be "the final abode of goodness."

According to the Mythology of Love, the Hero is not a special person. Instead, every individual, male or female without distinction or discrimination, is a special person—every individual is the Messiah. But the Hero is unique in that upon confronting the vision of the cathedral authority, clouded—as it can be—by fear, ignorance or pride, that Hero obeys the individual "heart" and thus obeys our will to love. The Hero's reward for having achieved such redemption is crucifixion—or alienation. If the cathedral authority is similarly redeemed, the alienation of the Heroic individual is eased, and the land laid waste by the absence of love begins to blossom, once again, with the promise of life. But if the cathedral authority is not redeemed, the crucifixion of the Hero will continue. Under such conditions the forces of chaos, as opposed to the forces of order, will rule the land.

In one of the great ironies of our Christian era, the cathedral it spawned has contributed to, and even continues—oftentimes with the noblest of intentions—the crucifixion of its World Savior. But the "biblical myth" of Christianity, when we read it from the inspiring Jungian perspective, in opposition to the more popular Freudian vision, illuminates the path of responsibility and salvation. In the post-moonwalk era of Western civilization we have little excuse for remaining ignorant of that path. And the longer we allow it to go undiscovered, the longer we will live in sin as we continue to lay waste the land we are supposed to create instead.

Amidst his thoughts on "The Stages of Life," Dr. Jung asks the question: "Do we understand what we think?" He answers that question by replying that "we only understand that thinking which is a mere equation, and from which nothing comes out but what we have put in. That is the working of the intellect." Our intellect calculates the rational, and we understand "that thinking which is a mere equation." As the "scientific discovery of ancient wisdom," and surpassing any thought that is a "mere equation," Jung's vision reflects behavior that individuals have continually exhibited but never have fully understood. By its very nature this inspiring thought is not divorced from experience. On the contrary, it holds little value when we separate it from that foundation. It then has no support and defies any calculation. As a result, we can easily overlook it and judge it to be unworthy of rational consideration—or we can promote it without proper understanding of its experiential, mythological foundation and turn it into a trendy psychology of convenience. And to turn Jung's convictions into popular convenience only adds fuel to the rationalist fire and lends further credibility to Freud's competing assessment of individual potential.

However, as Jung tells us, there is thinking beyond "the working of the intellect. Beyond that, there is thinking in primordial images—in symbols which are older than historical man." Furthermore, these symbols "have been ingrained in him from earliest times, and, eternally living, outlasting all generations, still make up the groundwork of the human psyche." If Jung's conclusions represent merely wish fulfillment of some kind, we could find little or no hope for humankind in the post-moonwalk era, and we would have no reason to echo the conviction William Faulkner revealed in his 1950 Nobel Prize Address. Faulkner "declined to accept the end of man" because he knew that the individual has a soul, "a spirit capable of compassion and sacrifice and endurance." Because of that soul, Faulkner believed that the individual would not "merely endure" but that he or she would "prevail." And the nature of that soul, that "spirit capable of compassion and sacrifice and endurance"—adding up to love—more often than not has been communicated through "primordial symbols—in symbols which are older than historical man." Jung's "historical man" gives expression to the "primordial images" through mythology, inclusive of religion and literature—through "the arts and particularly religious arts."

The crucifix is such a "primordial image." But it has no affective life when we read it as a provincial symbol of Christian atonement in a scientific age whose discoveries have discredited the supporting foundation of original sin and "mythic dissociation." Still, a "primordial image" is "eternally living." It outlasts "all generations" and "still makes up the groundwork of the human psyche." It represents the essence of the "psyche," of the soul, and thus the essence of the individual human being. When we read our symbol of the crucifix for what it is, a "primordial image" having nothing to do with any sin in any garden anywhere, we discover that essence to be love and nothing else. Free from the influence of original sin and from that of the Freudian psychological school—and even from that of the popular, convenient Jungian school—we can discover love that reveals the "human heart," and no institutional heart, whether ecclesiastical or secular, to be "the final abode of goodness."

The love that defines the "human heart" is not the Agape of the cathedral authority, still holding fast to its twin doctrines of "mythic dissociation" and original sin. Instead, it is the timeless Amor of the Hero, still embracing the "monstrous nature of life" that all authentic religion affirms. Art, and "particularly religious arts," is born out of that affirmation which we discover only when we are free from the visionary constraints of the cathedral doctrine. If we seek to live the "goodness" that is the "human heart," we seek to live the "life furthering ends" expressed in the "imageries of mythology and religion." We are not doomed to freedom as the Sartrean existentialists would have us believe. Rather, we are destined for it, and the liberating discoveries of our scientific age, combined with the enlightening results of celestial exploration, only further that cause of destiny. The imagery of mythology and religion, evidenced by the example of the crucifix, only springs to life when we acknowledge—and accept—the significance of our scientific triumphs.

Those triumphs have uncovered neither a subterranean Kingdom of Hell nor a celestial Kingdom of Heaven, which only confirms the "suspicion" that the "biblical myth" of Christianity is "historically" and physically "untrue." If the complementary Kingdoms of Hell and Heaven are not physically discovered kingdoms, they certainly are undiscovered psychological kingdoms that we create for ourselves while we live. And the call of Heaven resonates from the living crucifix, one of the "primordial images," one of the "symbols which are older than historical man; which have been ingrained in him from earliest times, and, eternally living, outlasting all generations, still make up the groundwork of the human psyche." And as Dr. Jung concludes: "it is only possible to live the fullest life when we are in harmony with those symbols." When we "live in harmony" with the symbol of the crucifix, we live to help create the Kingdom of God on earth. When we live otherwise, we live to help create the opposing Kingdom of Hell.

The ultimate, mythological majesty and promise of the cathedral, symbolic as it is of past glory, is no match for the immediate economic majesty and promise of the shopping mall. But if the days before the triumphs of rational science and the penetrating insights of celestial exploration saw the unparalleled majesty of the cathedral, the days following those triumphs and insights can see the unparalleled majesty of the individual. We can live in accord—in "harmony"—with the imagery of mythology and religion that is supposed "to serve positive, life furthering ends." Because we are beings capable of curiosity, wonder and obedience, we can discover for ourselves—in the spirit of the explorers and inventors who have preceded us—"the human heart as the final abode of goodness." If we discover and live the "goodness" that is the "human heart," we will do all we can to help create the Kingdom of God on earth. The earthly Kingdom of God is not the Agape Kingdom proclaimed by the cathedral pulpit in response to the economic challenge posed by the shopping mall and any rational, political system. Instead, that Kingdom is a Kingdom of Amor, a Kingdom of Individuals—male and female without distinction or discrimination—living their capacity to be God as expressions of the Word Made Flesh. It is an earthly Kingdom of Amor where individuals, standing tall and proud in all their existential majesty, live in obedience to the "human heart" as the "final abode of goodness." It is an earthly Kingdom of Amor carved out of the necessary "monstrous nature of life" by free, Heroic individuals—free to live their destiny as incarnations of the Word that lives in every "human heart" and free to refresh the land laid waste by its "hollow men" and "men of straw."

7

Baseball: America's Universal Game

During the course of our historical emergence on earth, covering hundreds of thousands of years, we haven't managed to create an orderly world of various peoples and cultures united by a common understanding of universally shared ideas. Instead, we have created a chaotic world of misunderstanding—and even fear—that can appear even more dangerous due to the very technological prowess that characterizes our scientific age. Even with the collapse of the Soviet Empire and the end of the Cold War, nuclear weaponry—with its possible discriminate or indiscriminate use—remains a threat. In addition, we only have to glance at our political and economic worlds, whether founded on capitalist or Marxist principles, to recognize the chaos that characterizes changing times and conditions. But this chaos also pervades the less immediate, though just as real, spiritual or mythological realm that continues to separate our Western world from that of the still mysterious East. However, in the midst of this political, economic and mythological chaos baseball emerges as America's universal game and, in the process, highlights the common spiritual, mythological foundation that unites West and East and—ultimately—the human race.

Mythological concerns, expressed in any form, appear to be irrelevant in a world overwhelmingly dominated by their economic counterparts. Still, we are more likely to search for meaningful expressions of God in the fields of music, literature or religion than we are in the world of sport. And if for some reason we, as American expressions of the Western individual, decided to conduct such a search in the world of sport, we would look at football before we would look at baseball. But sport as an art form, even if we don't understand it as such and even as we gasp at the breath-taking salaries commanded by our celebrity athletes, remains—primarily—an expression of mythological concerns. And in the world of sport, whether given Western or Eastern expression, baseball is unique because it isn't governed by time. Because it's free from the constraints of the clock, baseball is free to be naturally mythological and, therefore, just as naturally universal.

In 'The Firmament of Time' Dr. Eiseley distinguishes between what he terms "evolutionary time" and "purely durational time." Sports that are directly, or indirectly, governed by time—by the ticking of a clock or by the accumulation of points that ultimately determines the winner and thus the end of the game—are "durational" by nature. Football, for example—whether American or European style—is "durational" because of its dependency on the clock. In football we always face the danger of running out of time. Tennis and volleyball are examples of sports that appear to be free from the demands of time, but the end of a tennis or volleyball match is determined by one player, or one team, having attained the number of points it takes to win and thus to end the game. Golf and bowling most closely approximate baseball, but the golfer runs out of holes and the bowler runs out of frames. Only baseball is truly "evolutionary" and free from "durational" restraints because only baseball is governed by outs rather than by points, holes or frames. Three outs—not three minutes, three hours, three points, three holes or three frames—determine the end of an inning. In fact, the ultimate inning would be that in which the third out never is made, thus allowing the inning and the game to continue forever without any sense of "duration."

Dr. Eiseley's "evolutionary time," first discovered in the Christian West in the 18th century as part of the development of rational science, is the time of nature and thus the time of natural experience. On the other hand, "durational time" runs contrary to nature and its laws which means that any human creation governed by it runs contrary to the Laws of Nature. Mythology, which is born out of natural experience, represents our expression of these laws and is, therefore, "evolutionary" and for all time rather than "durational" and for a time. We created baseball, and because it is "evolutionary" in structure, it lives—as a result—in accord with the Laws of Nature. Therefore, baseball is mythology and an authentic expression of nature's laws born out of our natural experience. The various mythological expressions of the universal and eternal Laws of Nature look different, but if one "looks long" in keeping with the Chinese discipline of "wu-wei," that Joseph Campbell identifies in "The Inspiration of Oriental Art" from 'Myths to Live By,' "things will open up of themselves, according to their nature." Accordingly, if we "look(s) long" at the various mythological expressions of the Laws of Nature, we can discover the same laws revealed through a variety of "costumes." In this manner American baseball, given its "evolutionary" stature, can be a universal game because all of us—not just Eastern or Western individuals—live "evolutionary time" as children of nature.

In accord with "evolutionary time" we are not separate from nature, and with its acceptance, supported by thousands of years of experience as well as by the discoveries of rational science, comes the Western virtue of patience expressed, in the East, as the Chinese discipline of "wu-wei." Where time is thought to be "purely durational" there is no evidence of the manifestation of this virtue. Western scientists, led by geologist James Hutton in the 18th century, consciously discovered "evolutionary time" with their discovery of the antiquity of the earth that far surpassed the 4,000 years or so authorized by the Bible, the Christian revealed record of "purely durational time." The Western world, spiritually—or mythologically—governed by institutional Christianity since the fifth century, has lived, and continues to live, as though "evolutionary time" were "purely durational," thereby affecting a spiritual and psychological division between West and East. In reality, however, this division doesn't exist in light of the discovery and acceptance of "evolutionary time" as the time in which all humankind must live, given our universal identity as children of nature. Given our preponderance of Golden Arches, KMarts, roller coaster scream machines, wild wave water slides and centralized, suburban shopping malls, America—the leader of the Western capitalist world—is the most impatient of the Western countries. Therefore, it is most ironic that baseball, the very personification of the virtue of patience and of the Chinese discipline of "wu-wei," should have emerged and flourished in its cities and throughout its countryside.

America is impatient partly because it has emerged as the scientific leader of the West, leading the continuing journey outward in the name of progress that Dr. Eiseley identifies as the "endless movement of pursuit." But America is impatient primarily because it is fundamentally a biblical nation whose churches, contrary to the evidence of natural experience and the discoveries of rational science, continue to authorize "purely durational time" as being the truth. Therefore, we Americans read religion—if we choose to read it at all—as being something given to individuals by their Creator—by God. We don't read it in the manner of "evolutionary time" as being something we have given to ourselves out of recognition of natural, experiential truth only recently—the last 200 years being recent—verified by scientific discovery. For Americans, then, God is a "durational" being who can be found in a "durational" reading of religion and in its rational equivalent which, in the American world of sport, is the "durational" game of football.

However, the "evolutionary" game of baseball emerges as the universal game because the evidence of natural experience and the discoveries of rational science combine to authorize "evolutionary time," rather than "purely durational time," as the truth—the universal truth on which individuals, identified with either East or West, should base their lives. In the Age of Rational Science baseball is both the game of natural experience and the game of science. It is alternately the most primitive game and the most modern of games, reflecting both the experiential and rational nature of human beings. Because baseball is universal in nature, it gives expression to what Joseph Campbell would call "timeless universals" with the most "timeless" of all "universals" being the concept of God. As the personification of patience, baseball is not a reflection of the Old Testament Yahweh who exhibits no patience. But it is an expression of the New Testament Christ who, like the game itself, personifies patience. If Christ is patience and if Christ is the New Testament expression of God, then God is patience. It follows, therefore, that if God is patience and if baseball is patience, baseball is God. Thus baseball certainly is a "true" sport—if not The One True Sport.

When we see God as the personification of the virtue of patience, rather than as a male personality separate from us, the same God emerges both in the West and in the East. The Bible then becomes the Christian individual's, and not a separate God's, revealed, experiential truth of the psychological transformation of the Old Testament Yahweh, the Hebrew tribal God, into the New Testament Christ, the Christian expression of the Universal God. Like the Bhodisattvas of the Eastern Buddhist tradition, Christ remains in the world to teach the World Wisdom of Experience. Thus God has to be freed from "durational time" to become the authentic, Universal God of "evolutionary time." As long as we, as Western individuals, remain trapped in "durational time," we can't live our capacity to be God—with the psychological transformation of the tribal Yahweh into the New Testament Christ being an ancient projection, onto the world of time, of the timeless transformation of the individual from the state of the infantile ego to that of the adult ego. The adult ego is measured in terms of "evolutionary" rather than "durational" time, making American football—"durational" in nature—an expression of the infantile ego that grants its coaches the authoritative status of Yahweh. In contrast, baseball—being "evolutionary" in nature—remains an expression of the adult ego that grants its managers the experiential status of Christ, the Bhodisattva in whom one can find World Wisdom. Thus baseball is America's universal game able to bridge the gap we've created over the years that separates West from East.

The ensuing atmosphere of spiritual and mythological chaos has prevented us from recognizing the ultimate unity of humankind shaped around a common experience with God expressed in a variety of local, or what Joseph Campbell refers to as "ethnic," "costumes." In 'The Way of the Animal Powers' Campbell refers to Adolf Bastian—"world traveler as well as a major ethnologist of the 19th century"—who in the course of his travels discovered "in the myths and ceremonial customs of mankind a significant number of essential themes and motifs that were apparently universal." He termed these universal themes "ELEMENTARGEDANKEN" or as Mr. Campbell says "elementary ideas." Bastian also discovered that these "elementary ideas" were "clothed always in local forms" which he termed "VOLKERGEDANKEN," or "ethnic ideas." The most "elementary" of his "ELEMENTARGEDANKEN" is that of God. And when we see God, as expressed in the New Testament Christ, as a personification, an incarnation, of the universal virtue of patience—rather than as a separate, male personality—baseball becomes a local or "ethnic" expression of an "elementary idea."

Baseball certainly qualifies as an American "ceremonial custom." More specifically, as our national pastime, it is the American "ceremonial custom," which makes it even more troubling to witness the popular elevation of football to the level of religion. Because football is wedded to the ticking of the clock, it is more suited to the contemporary, "durational" lifestyle, but the more "durational" we become, the more separated we are from the Universal God of Experience personified in both baseball and Christ. Elevating the "durational" game of football to the level of religion—at the expense of the "evolutionary" game of baseball—further reveals the fundamental misunderstanding that continues to separate the West from the East. In addition, as we have elevated football to its lofty status, we have managed to dilute religion in the West—in the name of reform—and have only widened the gap with the East. In consequence we have seen numerous examples of disenchanted Westerners looking Eastward in search of the necessary spiritual, or mythological, dimension of life.

Because we have failed to acknowledge the significance of our psychological existence, following Jung's "scientifically rediscovered" thought, we find it easy to elevate football to the level of religion and to dilute the substance of Christianity at the same time. The emergence of rational science in the 18th century, continuing into the 21st century and beyond, proves that mythology—once accepted as a record of scientific fact—is indeed scientifically false instead. As result, the Western individual has witnessed the rational dilution of sacred "ceremonial customs"—mythological in nature—whether in the name of entertainment with regards to baseball or in the name of reform with regards to Christianity. But when we look "long" at those diluted "ceremonial customs," with the curiosity of a child awakened by the wondrous discoveries of rational science, Adolf Bastian's persuasive suggestions concerning "elementary" and "ethnic" ideas can more closely resemble scientific fact. Baseball then, as an expression of the scientific fact of "evolutionary time," rightfully earns the status of religion, living—as it does and unlike football—in complete accord with the scientific knowledge of the era.

Mythology then, though scientifically inaccurate, certainly isn't false. On the contrary, when we read it with curious eyes that take us beyond the boundaries once created by isolation, tradition and even institutional bigotry, its truth finally emerges in support of Jung's contention that "mythology expresses life more precisely than does science." To live in accord with mythology and baseball, both "evolutionary" in nature, is to live in accord with the natural truth that can bridge any gap that separates West and East. Furthermore, if we can live that natural truth, we can illuminate the nature of life itself and "more precisely" than can science alone. In the final analysis, science without mythology doesn't reflect life any more than does mythology without science.

It's easy, although not fair, for us to project the blame for any existing chaos onto science. In reality, however, we only have ourselves to blame. In the West—and all in the name of progress—we can forsake our mythology, as related to the world of "God," and embrace science, as related to the world of "Caesar," missing out on life in the process. Meanwhile, the East can forsake the creative influence of Western science to hold onto their mythological traditions and manage to miss out on life as well. When neither West nor East lives life expressed "precisely" through a scientific reading of mythology, the psychological, philosophical gap that divides West and East still exists and even can appear wider than ever. However, when we, as American expressions of the Western individual, "look long" at baseball and at Christ with the very virtue of patience personified in both, we can recognize that the unity of humankind—built around a common experience with God—definitely is possible. When we read mythology in terms of "evolutionary time," rather than in terms of "purely durational time," it comes alive with the promise of what could be, further solidifying baseball's status as mythology. After all, the game itself, free from the constraints of any clock, is solidly built on that promise. In baseball, in mythology, in "evolutionary time," hope truly "springs eternal in the human breast."

Our contemporary world, Western or Eastern, could use such authentic hope now and in the decades and centuries to come. The physical destruction of life, thanks to the presence of nuclear weapons, remains a possibility, and we've witnessed the waning of the power and influence of institutional authority, in the form of both church and state. But out of the resulting chaos we can discover the possibilities for the regeneration of human life. Therefore, we can serve our best interests by growing into baseball—our universal game that serves as an expression of the common, experiential God that psychologically, philosophically and spiritually unites the human race. Beneath the layers of decadence we have heaped upon it as part of the rational dilution of our "ceremonial customs," baseball remains a game of patience and thus a game of God with universal implications. As long as it remains free from the constraints of the clock, baseball always will be, essentially, a primitive game of patience and a sophisticated mythology of God that—when we read it scientifically—"expresses life more precisely than does science."

The continued rational dilution of God in the name of entertainment or reform will serve only to separate the Western individual further from the authentic God of Experience. We can find that God, which isn't limited to any local, tribal or "ethnic" identity, in "evolutionary time," rather than in "purely durational time." Thus when we see the human race as always having been a product of "evolutionary time"—following baseball's example—all distinction and discrimination fades away, leaving us with various "ethnic" expressions of "elementary" ideas. In fact, any individual man or woman becomes an "elementary" idea in that his or her spiritual and psychological nature emerges as being universal, or "archetypal" as Jung might say. Baseball is one, local, or "ethnic," expression of this universality. Therefore, like any other such expression, it can—and does—illuminate the path of understanding and maturation anyone can take to work toward the creation of the spiritual, psychological and philosophical unity that could be.

We can't blame science for the mythological chaos that marks our 21st century, but we can blame our own ignorance of the nature of life. We in the West have lived with the notion that ignorance is bliss, and the "durational" reading of our creation myth—the Garden of Eden story—has supported that contention. According to that reading, Adam and Eve sinned by choosing to eat the apple and leave the Garden of Paradise. If such a reading of the Eden story were true, generations of men and women, obediently avoiding that original sin, would have created a Western world characterized by order rather than by our contemporary chaos. The "durational" reading of Western Christianity, at the very least, is obsolete, and by continuing to live such a reading, we contribute—however unconsciously—more to the destruction of life than to its creation. The "evolutionary" reading of our creation myth, stressing the fact that Adam and Eve obediently avoided sin by choosing to eat the apple, is much more consistent with the experiential and scientific knowledge of our era. By eating the apple we embark on the path leading toward individuation and the accumulation of wisdom which, in turn, leads to authentic bliss and reinforces the words of

Christ—Christianity's expression of the archetypal World Teacher—who proclaimed: "Be ye therefore wise as serpents, and harmless as doves."

With the exception of its Muslim contingent, the East hasn't read its mythology as an expression of "durational time" in the manner of the West, but it, including the Islamic world, has been wedded to tradition. That wedding has helped prevent the East from discovering innovative readings of its mythological heritage that could release its individuals from any bondage to tradition and social roles—in much the same manner that the "evolutionary" reading of the West's mythological heritage releases its individuals from any bondage to institutional, ecclesiastical authority. This slavery to tradition in the East and to authority in the West has helped prevent the accomplishment of what Jung, in his autobiography, refers to as "reforms by retrogressions." In this instance we can measure such "reform" through an enlightened, scientific reading of mythology that serves to identify and free us from any bondage of which, willingly or unwillingly, we may be the victims. Baseball isn't necessarily the vehicle we need to facilitate this "reform by retrogression" by any means, but a patient look at something seemingly as frivolous as America's universal game reveals the ultimate, potential results of such authentic "reform."

The human race's historical emergence on this planet has created what Jung would call "dividing walls," and, curiously, these "walls" remain with us in the Age of Rational Science. In bygone eras, lacking in sophisticated communication systems and convenient modes of travel, we could be excused for failing to see beyond our "walls." In fact, Joseph Campbell, in his essay "Envoy: No More Horizons" from 'Myths to Live By' argues that:

> In earlier times, when the relevant social unit was the tribe, the religious sect, a nation, it was possible for the local mythology in service to that unit to represent all those beyond its bounds as inferior, and its own, local inflections of the universal human heritage of mythological imagery as the one, the true, and the sanctified, or at least as the noblest and supreme. And it was in those times beneficial to the order of the group that its young should be trained to respond positively to their own system of tribal signals and negatively to all others, to reserve their love for at home and to project their hatreds outward.

Today, reserving "love for at home" and projecting "hatreds outward," supported by our contemporary technological weaponry, is obsolete. In our time the "relevant social unit" no longer is "the tribe, the religious sect" or even "a nation." For us the "relevant social unit" is the universal family of human beings as inhabitants of the same planet whose health and survival depends on each individual living his or her responsibility to accept and live the dictates of "evolutionary time." Given this universal family's inevitable emergence as the "relevant social unit," baseball is only important for what it reveals as a "local inflection of the universal human heritage."

But Jung also states, and a patient look at America's "ceremonial custom" supports the contention, that "the dividing walls are transparent." And as Campbell adds in his editor's prologue to 'The Portable Jung': "where insight rules beyond differences, all pairs-of-opposites come together." Ours is not the time for "differences," or "indifferences," to rule. The "horizons" of past generations are gone forever, and today's young are growing into a world radically different from that which produced their parents and grandparents. "Differences" could rule in those "earlier times," but "insight" has to rule in the current and future times of their generation and of the generations that will follow in "evolutionary time." Individuals and their institutional structures can teach "insight," instead of "differences," to work—purposefully—toward the creation of life rather than—mistakenly—toward its destruction. "The program for life's morning," where "differences" ruled in a way "beneficial to the order of the group," is inadequate for "the afternoon of life." The "afternoon" demands to be ruled by "insight" that recognizes the "transparent" nature of our varied, colorful and once "dividing" walls.

The continuing historical emergence of humankind, covering the course of hundreds of thousands of years, does not have to result in the "end of man"—mythological or otherwise—or of the planet itself. If we measure our lives, and that of our planet, in "evolutionary time" rather than in "purely durational time" in both West and East—following the example of baseball rather than that of football—then hope truly "springs eternal in the human breast." Such romance is reminiscent of Nick Carraway's "green light" in F. Scott Fitzgerald's "evolutionary" and "insightful" classic 'The Great Gatsby':

> Gatsby believed in the green light, the orgiastic future that year by year recedes before us. It eluded us then, but that's no matter—tomorrow we will run faster, stretch out our arms farther And one fine morning—.

Embracing the experiential wisdom of the grizzled ballplayer, the experiential wisdom of "evolutionary time," all of us—from the West and East—can be ruled by "insight' rather than by "differences." Then we can "stretch out our arms farther" toward the promise of what could be "and one fine morning—."

8

Indian Yoga and the Psychology of Western Creative Mythology

From the dawning of our Age of Exploration to the flowering of our Age of Rational Science, we Westerners always have been intrigued by the mysteries of the East. At the height of our Columbian Age of Exploration the East—India especially—was an exotic land of wealth and romance capable of awakening both our capacity for exploitation and wonder. And now, steeped in our Age of Rational Science and embracing the 21st century, the East—India especially—remains that same exotic land with the power to awaken those same capacities. During our Columbian Age, we, as God's chosen people, exploited the material wealth of the East and India and wondered at the continued discovery of a people standing outside the boundaries of God's chosen family. Similarly, during our current Age of Rational Science, and with the existence of our separate God and Father discredited—or at least threatened—by our subsequent discoveries, we continue to exploit the spiritual wealth of the East and India. And we continue to wonder at the discovery of an inward life seemingly alien to our outwardly directed Western mind.

Spiritually bereft amidst the glitter of our scientific accomplishments and searching for the missing dimension of life—Jung's 'Modern Man in Search of a Soul'—we can either ignorantly adopt, or naively follow, the exploitive gurus—both native and imported—of Eastern spirituality. Removed from its natural environment and from its unique experiential foundation, this Eastern spirituality, or "Neo-Buddhism or Neo-Hinduism" as religious philosopher Alan Watts refers to it in 'The Supreme Identity,' can degenerate into, as Mr. Watts continues, "nothing more than rationalism and sentimentalism dressed up in misapplied Sanskrit terminology." Therefore, if we are to search for our lost soul, we have to search for reflections of the wondrous and mysterious Eastern spirituality in our own Western sources. Intrigued by the mystery of Indian Yoga, for example, we can explore it in comparison to our own mythological heritage to discover the common psychological foundation of Eastern and Western spirituality.

In his essay "The Inspiration of Oriental Art" taken from 'Myths to Live By,' Joseph Campbell identifies "the greatest works of the great periods of India" as "actually revelations" and continues by declaring that they are revelations "not of supposed supernatural beings, but of a power latent in ourselves and requiring only to be recognized to be brought to fulfillment in our lives." As "revelations" these "greatest works of the great periods of India" emphasize "fulfillment" here and now rather than in the irrevocable past or in some supposed future. This idea can be foreign to us, as expressions of the modern, rational individual, only because we have failed to recognize the significance of our own creative heritage. Specifically, we have failed to recognize "the Hero with a thousand faces" as representing our own revelation of that "power of nature latent in ourselves" that when recognized can "be brought to fulfillment in our lives." We can explore our own literature and religion—our own "creative mythology"—and discover the soul that is the inspiration both of Eastern and Western creative "revelations."

If we have acknowledged the significance of our "revelations" in any way, operating under the influence of the fundamental Christian premise of "mythic dissociation," we have seen the Hero as being separate from ourselves. Therefore, we never have recognized either literature or religion—"creative mythology"—as being the vehicles by which that power is awakened. Furthermore, we simply had no need to recognize this power of our religion and literature as long as we could believe in the fundamental separation of God and His creations. However, that premise, in light of the impressive discoveries of rational science, has lost its power to affectively direct our lives. As a result, we can wander aimlessly in our rational world without our God and with only the combined promise of economics and science to feed our aspirations.

But the very existence of mythology, either Eastern or Western and inclusive of both religion and literature, supports the existence of the imagination. It stands to reason, then, that we should read a product of the imagination, a product of the psyche to use the technical term, as an expression of that which produced it in the first place. To read mythology any other way is to misread it, to misunderstand it and, ultimately, to misdirect any power it may possess. Governed by the authoritative reading of our Christian Mythology, built on the premise of "mythic dissociation," we always have directed our energy "out there" in the direction of our separate God. As a result, we haven't read our mythology as an outward expression of our inward—or psychological—identity. Whatever contact we had with this inward, psychological identity, what Alan Watts would call "the supreme identity," had to be accidental and unconscious. But with the doctrine of "mythic dissociation" discredited, and with our resulting reliance on outward, scientific miracles, we can lose our accidental, unconscious contact with our "supreme identity." Thus we can immerse ourselves in our outward life, and having lost faith in our expressions of Western spirituality, we can turn to the East in search of the inward life we need to maintain that contact and experience fulfillment.

But there is danger to seeking fulfillment in the East at the expense of the West. In 'Creative Mythology' Joseph Campbell explains with a quote from Dr. Jung:

> A man does not sink down to beggary only to pose afterward as an Indian potentate. It seems to me that it would be far better stoutly to avow our spiritual poverty, our symbol-lessness, instead of feigning a legacy to which we are not the legitimate heirs at all.

We are not the "legitimate heirs" to Eastern spirituality, expressed in Indian yoga, for example. To pose, then, "as an Indian potentate" is to desecrate that spirituality and reduce it to "nothing more than rationalism and sentimentalism dressed up in misapplied Sanskrit terminology." We are, however, as Jung continues "the rightful heirs of Christian symbolism." And the "greatest works of the great periods" of Western civilization are reflections of that legacy, and the Hero, regardless of any individual "face," represents the concrete manifestation of the "symbolism" that presents our own expression of the individual's "supreme identity."

When we read it as a product of our inward nature, as a product of the psyche, the psychology reflected in Western creative mythology—focusing on the Hero—parallels the psychology expressed in Indian yoga and reveals the common soul that ultimately unites Eastern and Western individuals. As we learn from "The Inspiration of Oriental Art," to appreciate "the greatest works of the great periods of India"—and thus to appreciate their Western counterparts as "revelations of a power of nature latent in ourselves and requiring only to be recognized and brought to fulfillment in our lives"—we need only to consult the appropriate "psychological textbook." For Joseph Campbell that appropriate text is "that extraordinary psychological textbook, 'A Description of the Six Bodily Centers of the Unfolding Serpent Power' (Shatchakra-nirupanum) available in the superb translation of Sir John Woodroffe."

Indian Yoga and the Psychology of Western Creative Mythology

Indian yoga appears alien to Western thought only because we've never considered our "great works" from our "greatest periods" to be records of inward, psychological experience. If anything, we've considered them to be records of outward, historic and scientific fact only to lose faith in them when we discover—as a result of our natural experience with life—that they aren't historically and scientifically true. In the process, we've identified both the Hero and God as being both separate from ourselves and from each other. Our belief and faith in our Hero is only as strong as our belief and faith in our God. Therefore, to our outwardly directed mind, Indian yoga, as an inward experience, has to be an alien and mysterious practice. And with our fundamental premise of "mythic dissociation"—as it applies to both the Hero and God—discredited through rational explanation, naturally accumulated experience and the discoveries of contemporary science, the adventure can be most attractive. Thus we can turn to the East and Indian yoga in search of the mystery we've lost in our own lives. In so doing, we can fail to understand that our loss of faith in our traditional, historically based reading of our mythological heritage represents a necessary step on our journey to individual maturation. With the temporary light of innocence extinguished, we are now free to experience, and discover, the permanent light of maturity.

We can begin by seeing our own "greatest works of the great periods" as timeless, inward "revelations" projected outward onto the world of time. We can begin by examining our mythological heritage—inclusive of literature and religion—in relation to "that extraordinary psychological textbook" that examines the "six bodily centers of the unfolding serpent power." As Campbell explains in his essay on Oriental art:

> The basic thesis of this so-called Kundalini yoga system elucidated in this fundamental work is that there are six plus one—i.e., seven—psychological centers distributed up the body, from its base to the crown of the head, which can through yoga, be successfully activated and so caused to release ever higher realizations of spiritual consciousness and bliss.

For us to see this "basic thesis" only as an Eastern expression of an Eastern idea, somehow alien to our thought, we have to be inattentive to the world of experience populated by human beings living at various levels—or stuck on one level—of psychological awareness or psychological "consciousness." Like all great mythological, religious thought, the "basic thesis of this so-called Kundalini yoga system" has to be born out of experience. Thus it can be an Eastern expression of a more universal idea or an Eastern, "ethnic" expression of a universal, "elementary" idea.

For us to see "the basic thesis of the so-called Kundalini yoga system" as an "ethnic" expression of an "elementary" idea, we have to reconsider our traditional understanding of our mythological heritage. In our search for God, for example, we have to direct our attention away from our celestial terrain and toward our earthly terrain, focusing, this time, on the individual human being. If we direct our attention toward the individual, we can rediscover the God from whom we were alienated when the Orthodox version of Christianity, solidly built on the premise of "mythic dissociation," won the favor of Imperial Rome in the fifth century. With the Garden of Eden story—the foundation of Western Christianity—discredited as a record of historic and scientific fact, we are free from the influence of original sin and free from our subsequent need for redemptive atonement. For the first time, we are free to discover the Hero as being the incarnation of God who always has lived, as a psychic being, within the universal individual and thus within that individual's Western, "ethnic" expression.

In the Kundalini yoga system, following Joseph Campbell's description, the psychological centers "are known as 'lotuses' padmas, or as chakras 'wheels,' and are thought to be normally hanging limp." The idea behind the Kundalini terminology isn't alien to us when we examine our mythological heritage and see something that was made up to give expression to the truth of experience that, ultimately, turns out to be reinforced—rather than refuted—by the discoveries of rational science. If we accept our mythological legacy, inclusive of literature and religion, as being a product of the psyche, we can understand its function which is to project the timeless world of experience onto the world of time. As a result, we can recognize our psychological potential whose various levels, devoid of the necessary inspiration, can be thought to be, like their corresponding "'lotuses'" or "'wheels,'" "normally hanging limp."

The Indian expression of "a rising spiritual power called the Kundalini," that calls various "'lotuses'" or "'wheels'" to life, makes sense to us when we think of our own rediscovered psychological potential. Given our exhaustive exploration of our earthly and celestial terrain—from the age of Columbian sailors to the age of the Mercury, Gemini and Apollo astronauts—we easily can remain ignorant of our psychological terrain and its accompanying potential. We can remain ignorant of the "coiled serpent" that in India "is thought of as feminine, the feminine form-building, life-giving and supporting force by which the universe and all its beings are rendered animate." Kundalini is a "feminine Sanskrit noun" meaning "'the coiled one,'" and the Western Hero, stripped of its primarily masculine "face," reveals this feminine "life-giving and supporting force." The Hero is "animate" because essentially, regardless of any individual "face," he or she is the incarnation of love which is the Western, "ethnic" expression of the universal—and "elementary"—"life-giving and supporting force by which the universe and all its beings are rendered animate."

This abstract feminine power—whether termed Kundalini in the East or Love in the West and given concrete expression through the symbol of the "coiled serpent"—has the power to render all things "animate." But until it's awakened, it lies sleeping, as Campbell tells us, "in the lowest of the seven centers of the body," leaving "the other six unactivated." But once this Kundalini, or spiritual power of love, is activated, it is a constant, living force that stays in motion, rendering life to a being otherwise inert, lifeless and inanimate. Thus the "coiled serpent" has to be awakened before the inanimate human being can be rendered "animate." As Mr. Campbell continues:

> The aim, therefore, of this yoga is to wake the serpent, cause her to lift her head, and to bring her up the mystic interior channel of the spine known as Sushama, "rich in pleasure," piercing at each stage of her thrilling ascent the lotus there located.

Such is the aim of Western creative mythology as well, and such is the "affect power" of the Hero. The Hero has the power to "affect" the individual and awaken the "coiled serpent," provided the individual is willing to live Gottfried von Strassburg's "noble heart."

But we, as Western individuals, have lost sight of our "noble heart," rendering our "creative mythology" and our Hero powerless. The discoveries of our own rational science have discredited our traditional premise of "mythic dissociation," leaving us with no living expression of our mythological legacy. To our 21st-century, rational mind neither religion nor literature can be true because neither functions, primarily, as a source of rational, scientific and historic fact. In terms of our psychological potential, then, we live rational—but inanimate—lives. For the most part we live only at any one of the first three "'lotuses'" or "'wheels'" of this "unfolding serpent power." As a result, we live—primarily—in response to our will to pleasure or to power. With our "closed heart" we've yet to discover our will to love—Jung's "undiscovered self."

Psychologically, therefore, we live either with the "coiled serpent" resting "in the first lotus center asleep" in a state of what Campbell calls "spiritual turpor" or with the serpent having risen to "center number two, the level of the genitals or, finally, "lotus three" which is "at the level of the navel." Living at level one—the lowest of the seven body centers—we live the life of what Campbell identifies as that of a "creep" and, as he continues, "God knows such people are numerous enough." Living at level two, the "level of the genitals," we live at the level of pleasure in which "everything means sex to him." According to Mr. Campbell, this stage is "of a psychology perfectly Freudian" with Freud being certain "that there was nothing else people lived for." Living at level three, the level of the navel, we live at the level of power "where one's governing interest is in consuming, conquering, turning all into his own substance, or forcing all to conform to his way of thought." Following Campbell, once again, this psychology "ruled by an insatiable will to power is of an Adlerian type." After his concise analysis of the first three levels of this "unfolding serpent power" that can be applied to the contemporary, and rational, Western individual, Mr. Campbell concludes by saying:

> And so Freud and Adler and their followers can be said to have interpreted the phenomenology of the spirit in terms exclusively of chakras two and three—which is enough to explain their inability to make something more interesting either of the mythological symbols of mankind or of the goals of human aspiration.

If Freud and Adler are correct in their assessment of individual psychological potential and of individual, "human aspiration," the mythological legacy of the West, including our religion built around the figure of Christ as the Hero in one of a "thousand faces," is useless. In addition, if Freud and Adler are correct, the "Kundalini yoga system" is of absolutely no use to any of us as a tool to help us understand our own spiritual heritage. And most ominously of all, if Freud and Adler are correct, we are left only with science and whatever impetus it can contribute to our continuing quest for pleasure and power.

We recognize the popular influence of Freudian and Adlerian thought because we, as Western individuals, remain closed to the significance of the "mythological symbols of mankind." Thus we have little, and even no, knowledge or understanding of the majesty of "human aspiration." As a revelation inspired by experience, we created mythology by ourselves for ourselves. Therefore, the Hero of "creative mythology"—who never, regardless of any individual "face," lives at the level of the first, second or third "chakra"—is the myth-maker's expression of individual human potential observed first in the world of experience. The Hero is made up, but he or she is made up from experience and represents the myth-maker's conscious, or unconscious, expression of the truth of that experience. The myth-maker, then, is a child of experience who, as Shakespeare says, "gives to airy nothingness a local habitation and a name." In the Chinese spirit of "wu-wei," or "not doing," the myth-maker mainly "looks." And as we know, "one looks, looks long, and the world comes in. Things will open up of themselves, according to their nature."

The myth-maker follows that pattern, and the individual opens up of itself, according to his or her nature. Obviously, that nature, in both the male and female expression, reveals a capacity to seek pleasure and power not confined to Western individuals. And to make matters worse, with our "closed hearts" we can remain ignorant of our potential to live in response to something that takes us beyond those recognizable levels. But when we "look long," with the curious, penetrating eyes of the artist, we see the true nature of the individual human being, which turns out to be greater than what Freud and Adler saw. For whatever reasons, in interpreting "the phenomenology of the spirit in terms exclusively of chakras two and three," they failed to see, for example, the "great expectations" the eyes of a Charles Dickens recognized. They didn't "look long" in the manner of the artist, or myth-maker, and failed to see the noble, although oftentimes misguided, aspirations of which individual human beings are capable.

From the tragic quest of Pip in Dickens' 'Great Expectations' to the romantic quest of Odysseus, Adam and Eve, Christ or Huckleberry Finn, the Hero's journey—regardless of any individual "face"—is motivated more by love than by any desire for pleasure or power. If we "look long," we will discover that love—identified as Amor by the medieval troubadours—and recognize it as the "power of nature latent in ourselves." Until we discover and live this power, either consciously or unconsciously, we are inanimate because as Joseph Campbell explains in his analysis of the "Kundalini yoga system":

> For it is only at the level of the fourth chakra that specifically human, as distinct from sublimated animal aims and drives become envisioned and awakened; and, according to the Indian view, it is to this level and beyond (not to the concerns of chakras one, two, and three) that religious symbols, the imagery of art, and the questions of philosophy properly refer.

To Freud and Adler and their followers, then, "who have interpreted the phenomenology of the spirit in terms exclusively of chakras two and three," as individuals we cannot be noble, free and human. Instead, we only can live as slaves to "sublimated animal aims and drives." When we see ourselves only in the light of Freudian or Adlerian conclusions, we are either doomed by, or enslaved to, our miraculous Age of Rational Science.

But we can be free and "human." We have the experientially inspired work of the artist, or myth-maker, as well as the mythologically inspired thought of the Jungs and Campbells, to testify to that conclusion. In the world of what we can call "creative mythology" the separate disciplines of psychology, philosophy and religion come together to give common expression to our "specifically human" nature as "distinct from the sublimated animal aims and drives." This "specifically human" nature, an abstraction in itself, is given concrete expression in the Hero whose inherent "serpent power" has risen beyond the levels of "sublimated animal aims and drives"—"<u>chakras</u> one, two, and three." In so doing the Hero "with a thousand faces" functions as a "revelation" of the "power of nature latent in ourselves," as a "revelation" of Jung's mythologically inspired "undiscovered self." And, ultimately, the Hero functions as a "revelation," an incarnation, of what Western individuals—now free from the influence of original sin and the authoritative Christian doctrine of "mythic dissociation"—can identify as God.

Significantly, the lotus of this fourth "<u>chakra</u>" lives "at the level of the heart." The Hero of the pagan mythologies of the West, we remember, "moved by an infallible natural grace, follows without fear the urges of his heart." Furthermore, in his Nobel Prize Address Faulkner exhorts the modern artist to write "of the heart" and "not of the glands." And Jung's mythologically inspired thought identifies the "heart" as the symbolic expression of the unconscious that, he concluded, turns out to be "collective." Also, the "power of nature, latent in ourselves," that when awakened and lived makes us "human," lives in the heart. The "power of nature," our "infallible natural grace," as our "supreme identity," reveals the Self, the God that resides within us and is made Flesh in the person of the Hero regardless of any individual "face." We live that "power of nature," our "infallible natural grace," when we make the Word Flesh and live the Way of the Cross—each as a Christ, each as a living expression of the crucifix, the Western "religious symbol" that "has for its content the individual way of life of a man, the Son of Man." Western Christianity itself "holds at its core" this symbol and "even regards this individuation process as the incarnation and revelation of God himself."

Contrary to Freud and Adler, Jung did not interpret "the phenomenology of the spirit exclusively in terms of <u>chakras</u> two and three." Therefore, his thought—as revealed in 'The Undiscovered Self,' for example—is not characterized by the "inability to make anything more interesting either of the mythological symbols of mankind or of the goals of human aspiration." In fact, according to Jung:

> Great art till now has always derived its fruitfulness from the myth, from the unconscious process of symbolization which continues through the ages and which, as the primordial manifestation of the human spirit, will continue to be the root of all creation in the future.

So, the psychology we can recognize in Indian yoga and in our own Western creative mythology, is neither Freudian nor Adlerian. It is neither a psychology of pleasure nor one of power. Instead, it is a Jungian psychology of love where the symbol of the crucifix, for Western individuals, functions as the "primordial manifestation of the human spirit" which proves itself to be, essentially, not pleasure or power but love—Amor. The "great art" of India and the Orient and the "great art" of the West, that derives "its fruitfulness from the myth," therefore "lifts up mans' heart" as a result of the individual artist conscientiously fulfilling the responsibility Faulkner emphasized in his Nobel Prize Address. Thus when we view it with the proper curiosity and wonder, this "great art," this "creative mythological thought," springs from a common, experiential foundation—regardless of the "dicta of authority." As a result, it holds the key to the discovery of the ultimate psychological—and spiritual—unity of humankind.

We are faced with the challenge of discovering that common psychological and spiritual foundation. In our search for Hero, the symbolic expression of our common soul, we can start with Christ, our New Testament expression of God. In the process we can read him not primarily as an historic being trapped in time but rather as a psychological, "mythic" being projected onto time as a timeless reminder of the truth of our psychic potential and of our capacity to live "great expectations." We're free to read Christ as Hero, as a psychological, "mythic" being, because we're free from the constraining influence of original sin and its accompanying doctrine of "mythic dissociation." When we read Christ primarily as a mythic expression of an individual's potential for love, Amor—and not primarily as an historical expression of a dissociated God's love for His creations—he can function as the Hero in one of a "thousand faces." When we read him as a "mythic" being projected onto time as a product of the individual's psyche, he can function with the "affect power" of the Hero and inspire any "noble heart" to live beyond the levels of "chakras two and three," beyond our capacity for pleasure and power and at our capacity for love—for Amor. When we are inspired to live at the level of "chakra" four, we can begin to live our destiny as "incarnations and revelations of God himself."

But in our search for "satisfaction" amidst the comforts provided by science, we can desert our own rich heritage for that of the East because of our mistaken notion that our Western heritage has little or nothing to offer. If we look and "look long" in the Chinese manner of "wu-wei," or with the Western virtue of patience, we will find the spiritual or mythological dimension we seek in our own Western mythological heritage. If we "look long" with patience, we will find the "satisfaction" we need in our Western Hero and our Western expression of God. When we approach this fundamental, "elementary" idea with the necessary curiosity and wonder, God is revealed to be the inward, psychic being awakened by the "unfolding serpent power," and not the outward, physical being—not subject to any such awakening—we traditionally have accepted. When we "look long" with patience at our God, we discover "the power of nature latent in ourselves," the power of Amor—the "infallible natural grace" associated with the Western pagan Hero rediscovered by the medieval troubadours.

The "Kundalini yoga system" of India is designed to foster the release of "this power of nature latent in ourselves," and its counterpart in the West had to be the Catholic Mass whose sacred symbols, chants and language corresponded to the sacred symbols of Indian prayer and meditation. And when we saw that Mass in support of a mythological system based on the still-believable doctrine of "mythic dissociation," it could work its "affect" magic on any "noble heart" and awaken the "serpent power" that lives at the level of the heart otherwise latent or "hanging limp." But in our attempt to meet the scientific challenge of our era we diluted this sacred, symbolic expression of the "unfolding serpent power" when, instead of reforming the pulpit to reinforce the altar, we reformed the altar to reinforce the pulpit. In so doing we reduced the sacred, Western ritual expression of the universal "power of nature latent in ourselves" to words. And as Joseph Campbell reminds us in "The Confrontation of East and West in Religion," words "only serve to make you think you have understood."

Still, the Western Hero remains a part of the language of symbols waiting to be discovered consciously for the first time. If we can discover our Hero, we can discover our God because the Hero, in all its "thousand faces"—from the likes of Odysseus to the likes of Huckleberry Finn—is God. In the psychology of Western creative mythology, the Hero is the symbolic expression of "the feminine form-building, life-giving, and supporting force" that lies "latent" in Yahweh of the Old Testament but is given life through Christ in the New Testament. With the birth of Christ Yahweh is transformed into the authentic God and, in the person of Christ, emerges as a living expression of that "force," as an incarnation of the Word—what Campbell refers to as "the Word behind all Words"—made Flesh. Odysseus, as opposed to his fellow warrior, Achilles, discovers this "feminine, form-building, life-giving and supporting force"—the "power of nature latent in ourselves"—and in the process becomes a man worthy to be called king.

Huckleberry Finn discovers that same force and in obedience to it, even if neither he nor the Christian pulpit authority he had to disobey consciously realizes such, discovers God. Walking out into the rain at the end of Ernest Hemingway's 'A Farewell to Arms' after the death of his true love, Catherine, and their baby, Frederick Henry faces the beginning of his life with the recognition that, as Jake Barnes discovered in Hemingway's 'The Sun Also Rises,' "the bill always comes."

Likewise, the bill has come for us as Western individuals. In response to the inevitable waning of the power and influence of our institutional Christianity, we've reduced our mythology to the level of diversion and entertainment and have encouraged, perhaps unintentionally, the psychological behavior associated with "chakras two and three" in the "Kundalini yoga system" and with the conclusions identified with Freud and Adler in Western psychology. Upon facing the coming of "the bill," we've concluded, in the manner of Shakespeare's Macbeth, that "life is a tale told by an idiot full of sound and fury signifying nothing." But we have only encountered the darkness that follows the death of the temporary light. If Frederick Henry, at the beginning of his life, "looks" and "looks long" at the life of the Hero in the "face" of his true love, Catherine Barkley, he will discover the "feminine, form-building, life-giving supporting force by which the universe and all its beings are rendered animate." And if at the beginning of our life, we "look" and "look long" at the life of the Hero in the "face" of Christ as well, we, too, will discover that same "form-building, life-giving supporting force."

We will discover that "force," the "power of nature latent within ourselves," and unlike our experience in our initial life, we will discover that our God and Hero does not live in celestial or monastic "dissociation" at the level of "chakra" five "separate from art and civilized life." Rather, looking through the mythologically inspired eyes of Dr. Jung, we will discover that our God-Hero remains in the world as an "animate" force imbued with omniscience—measured in terms of wisdom and compassion—associated with "chakras" six and seven in the "Kundalini yoga system" and normally seen as being at a level "beyond art." In the psychology of Western creative mythology this God-Hero remains in the world like Christ as a teacher or like Huckleberry Finn and Catherine Barkley as quiet expressions of that "feminine form-building, life-giving supporting force by which the universe and all its beings are rendered animate." Wearing any one of a "thousand faces" in the world of literature and religion—the world of "creative mythology"—or in the concrete world of experience, this Western God-Hero, when discovered, carries the "affect power" to awaken any "noble heart."

But our "noble heart"—once subject to awakening more by accident than by design—lies dormant or inert or "hanging limp" in the language of the "Kundalini yoga system" of India. With our collective heart closed as a result of our loss of faith in our "creative mythology" as an affective force, we can, and do, live in ignorance of the "power of nature latent in ourselves." In so doing we can live in slavery to our science's deceptive promise of fulfillment in some still-to-be-realized future. But there is truth beyond science. Metaphysical, mythological truth can be realized by each individual here and now with the discovery of the Western God-Hero. In assessing the "phenomenology of the spirit" in accord with the mythologically inspired thought of the likes of Joseph Campbell and Carl Jung, we can discover—in our own mythology—that "feminine form-building, life-giving supporting force by which the universe and all its beings are rendered animate." We can discover the "supporting force" made Flesh in our God-Hero "with a thousand faces." In the process we can discover the common psychological foundation, and the common soul, that unites East and West. And because we will not have ceased to explore, to paraphrase T. S. Eliot, the end of all our exploration will be to arrive where we started and know ourselves for the first time.

9

An Answer to Carl Jung's "Answer to Job"

The 19th century of our Christian era witnessed the birth of the Industrial Revolution and the subsequent emergence of the science of psychology. Knowledge of what we routinely call the psyche today was not new to the 19th century, but the scientific discovery of it was. Becoming consciously aware of its role in the life of the individual represented a breakthrough every bit as significant as the invention and development of the steam engine that fueled the revolution itself. We didn't invent the steam engine until it was necessary to do so, and, similarly, we didn't scientifically discover the psyche until circumstances—specifically the Western world's inevitable transformation from an agrarian to an industrial society—demanded it. The psyche refused to be ignored as a result of the growing emphasis we placed on urban, industrial development often at the expense of natural, agrarian—and psychic—development. Given these circumstances, a curious thinker like Sigmund Freud proved to be the right man, at the right place and at the right time—as did his disciple, Carl Jung. But it was left to Jung, alive with wonder and curiosity that surpassed even that of his mentor, to discover the inspirational world of mythology and religion that, in turn, led him to write his 'Answer to Job.'

Jung's discovery was necessary because, as we remember from Joseph Campbell and 'Creative Mythology': "for not authority but aspiration is the motivator, builder, and transformer of civilization." Jung himself is a concrete example of this experiential wisdom because Freud's authority did not motivate him to speak and write of our capacity and potential to build and transform our society psychologically, from within, to keep pace with the building and transforming of our society industrially, from without. His curiosity and wonder took him beyond the boundaries his respected authority created and led him to discover the creative secrets of the mythological world. Alive with the spirit of building, creating and transforming, Jung studied the sacred scripture of the Christian Mythology, specifically the Book of Job from the Old Testament.

As we learn from 'Creative Mythology,' "a mythological canon is an organization of symbols, ineffable in import, by which the energies of aspiration are evoked and gathered toward a focus." Christianity is such an "organization of symbols," but when we read it historically and unscientifically, it is a "mythological canon" that no longer generates the power to awaken "the energies of aspiration" and therefore lacks the force to "gather them toward a focus." When we read it historically and unscientifically, Christianity lives up to Freud's assessment of it being an error "to be refuted, surpassed and finally supplanted by science." When we read it primarily as a history, complete with lessons, Christianity encourages suppression of the individual identity and will not suffice in an era that prides itself, however ignorantly or innocently, on individual expression. In the face of the psychologically inadequate reading of Christianity, we are left with the "mythological canons" associated with the likes of rock music and the shopping mall both of whose "organizations of symbols" clearly evoke "the energies of aspiration" and gather them "toward a focus."

For the adherents to such "mythological canons" the "authorized signs" of Christianity, or those of their local, family mythology, "no longer work." Or if they do work, they "produce deviant effects" as Campbell continues in 'Creative Mythology.' The "mythological canons" reflected in the likes of rock music and the shopping mall actually can lead their followers away from the individual path they seek, and because their "canons" aren't authentic, they are—by default—more coercive than evocative. Ironically, such coercive "canons" succeed only in hardening the individual, Campbell tells us, into "some figure of living death; and if any considerable number of the members of a civilization are in this predicament, a point of no return will have been passed." To avoid this "point of no return" and to perhaps "soften" into or to "blossom" into "some figure of living life," we can think about answering Jung's 'Answer to Job.'

To begin with, the Book of Job is the work of an artist, a "poet" as Faulkner might say, and not the work of an historian. Therefore, we should not read the work primarily as a record of historical fact. "The poet's voice," Faulkner says, "need not merely be the record of man; it can be one of the props, the pillars to help him endure and prevail." To answer Jung's 'Answer to Job,' we have to follow Faulkner's lead and approach the book as if it were more than "merely the record of man." As a history, as part of the mere "record of man," the Book of Job, like any other story, is irrelevant outside the boundaries of its historical time frame. What applied to Job then, as an historical being subject to his God, no longer applies to us, and what happened to Christ, as an historical being tempted in the desert, no longer applies either. Thus by reading mythology primarily as history, we render it irrelevant outside its particular historical era. It is then unable to guide anyone through the adventure of life, leading us, whether or not we realize it, to believe as did Huckleberry Finn who didn't "take no stock in dead people."

For us to "take stock" in Job, Christ or in any character from the mythological world, we must see them, and their companion characters, as being something more than figures from history. As such they are trapped in their time and are useless outside of its boundaries. They are reduced to merely representing part of the "record of man." But when we read them as Jung's psychological beings—as mythic beings—projected onto time, they're free from its restraints and become, as a result, for all time. When we read them as mythic beings, Job and his companion characters from the mythological world become immortal expressions of the "poet's voice" that is supposed to be "one of the props, the pillars to help him (man) endure and prevail." The world of mythology, inclusive of religion and literature, is the expression of the soul of humankind, whether or not the individual myth-maker consciously realizes it. As Faulkner explains, the artist—the "poet"—assumes the responsibility "to help man endure by lifting up his heart, by reminding him of the courage and honor and hope and pride and compassion and duty which have been the glory of his past." And the individual reader, watcher or listener assumes the responsibility to acknowledge the "poet's voice" as representing not merely "the record of man" but "one of the props, the pillars to help him endure and prevail."

If life weren't monstrous in nature, we would have no need for "props" or "pillars" to help us "endure" and "prevail." But the artist is a child of experience that, regardless of the historical conditions of any era, reveals Joseph Campbell's "monstrous nature of life." The artist's work, therefore, is born from his or her encounter with experience and emerges as a "record" of its truth, revealing in the process the path, the way, to the transcendence of both time and death. The artist is not a child of authority, and if authority's response to the monster doesn't reinforce reason and experience, he or she will live in alienation from it. The artist will obey authority until he or she outgrows it, in the manner of Jung following and then outgrowing Freud. Jung read the world of mythology, and, therefore, the Book of Job, as would an artist—as would a child of experience—free from the authoritative Christian doctrine that identifies the original sin of Adam and Eve in the Garden of Eden as the rational cause for the effect that is "the monstrous nature of life." For Jung and the artist, for the child of experience, life is naturally monstrous, and our recognition and affirmation of it prompts us to create mythology. Therefore, reading the Book of Job from experience, rather than from authority—in answer to Jung's 'Answer to Job'—offers a revelation that supports Faulkner's conviction that we "will not merely endure" but that we "will prevail."

When we read it from the position of authority, without the freedom that allows for curiosity and wonder, Yahweh in the Book of Job is the authentic God, separate from His creation, who later sent His only begotten Son, Jesus Christ, to earth—the historical Incarnation—to redeem the human race for having sinned in the Garden of Eden. We are redeemed through our obedience to Christ's Church, of which there are a multitude, that illuminates the path of atonement and eventual union with the Father upon completion of our earthly lives in this "vale of tears." This authoritative reading, however, presents the 21st century reader—and the readers of the centuries to follow—with at least two significant problems. First of all, the doctrine of "mythic dissociation" is untenable in light of the discoveries associated with modern science and celestial exploration. Secondly, the characteristics of "courage and honor and hope and pride and compassion and pity and sacrifice" are nowhere to be found in Yahweh who, as God, should personify those virtues. When we read it only from the position of authority, the Book of Job, with Yahweh as the authentic God and Creator of the Universe, makes no sense to the serious reader, whether living in the 21st century or beyond. We have the right to expect more than jealousy and rage and deceit and treachery and arrogance from our God.

However, when we read it from the position of experience, which allows for curiosity and wonder, the significant problems disappear—leaving only the revelation that always has been present. The experiential reading of the Book of Job offers the revelation that the individual human being can live as God. It offers the revelation that God exists more as psychic being inherent in the individual than as a physical being separate from His creation. In his prefatory note to his 'Answer to Job' Jung states that he will have "to speak of the venerable objects of religious belief" and continues by saying that "whoever talks of such matters inevitably runs the risk of being torn to pieces by the two parties who are in mortal combat about these very things." For Jung "this conflict is due to the strange supposition that a thing is only true if it presents itself as a <u>physical</u> fact" causing "some people to believe it to be physically true that Christ was born of a virgin" while causing others to "deny this as a physical impossibility." After adding that "both are right and both are wrong," Jung concludes that "they could easily reach agreement if only they dropped the word 'physical.'" We no longer enjoy the luxury of ignoring Jung's conclusion. The exploration of our celestial terrain, the discoveries of rational science and the triumph of philosophical reasoning at least strongly suggest, if they don't convincingly prove, that if God doesn't exist as a "psychic truth," he doesn't exist at all.

If faith in God were as strong today as at least it appeared to be in the decades prior to the last five years of the 1960s, the "mythological canons" associated with the likes of rock music and the shopping mall would not exert the influence they obviously do. But the 60s decade, particularly the last five years following the conclusion of the Second Vatican Council of the Roman Catholic Church, witnessed the collective loss of belief in the Garden of Eden story—the foundation of the Christian Mythology and of the Christian era of Western civilization. We have been reeling in chaos ever since because we haven't discovered, nor has our institutional church presented, Christianity as an expression of "psychic truth." Jung didn't have to live in the spiritual "Waste Land" of post-Vatican II Western civilization, but it he were to join us, he would see little hope if God isn't a "psychic truth" we all have the capacity to live. Otherwise, we would be doomed to wait for the "Godot" who never will show up. We inhabit a land reflecting the same "spiritual death" Joseph Campbell identifies in the Grail Legend of medieval Europe. And in our spiritual "Waste Land" each individual is the "Desired Knight who would restore its integrity to life and let stream again from infinite depths the lost, forgotten, living waters of the inexhaustible source."

Therefore, we don't have to wait for any "Desired Knight" to arrive and deliver us from the "Waste Land." In fact, to wait for that "Knight" is to wait in despair, leading to the final recognition that there is no "Desired Knight" in the first place. Then we can turn by default to the "mythological canons" associated with the likes of rock music and the shopping mall to gather "toward a focus" whatever "energies or aspiration" we may have left. Ironically, Christianity—when we read it primarily as a record of "physical truth"—contributes to this despair and desperation because it promises the return of the "Desired Knight" in the person of Christ—God or Godot—who hasn't returned for almost 2,000 years. After waiting so long, anyone—either privately or publicly—would have to begin to question the truth behind that promise. Two thousand years after His crucifixion, death, resurrection and ascension, the One True God—Lord and Creator of the Universe—has not returned to deliver His children from the "Waste Land." Clearly, the Messianic Age is upon us, and each individual, as a contributor to the "Waste Land," is the needed Messiah. If one man among individuals is God, then every individual—male and female—is God in support of the words of the God-Man of Christianity, Christ, who proclaimed: "I and my Father are one."

If we can perceive the Father as love and pity and compassion and honor and humility—and certainly any individual has the right to expect any father, historical or mythological, to make such words Flesh—the Book of Job tells us that the Father to whom Christ refers can't be the Yahweh who forces the obedient Job into humiliation. That same Yahweh commands Adam and Eve in the Garden of Eden to remain ignorant in obedience to Him because, as in the case of Job, without that devotion Yahweh ceases to exist. A Father who is supposed to be the incarnation of love, the Word Made Flesh, doesn't humiliate His children in the manner in which Yahweh humiliates Job. Nor does He command his children to remain ignorant and increasingly dependent on Him so as to ensure His existence as Lord and Master who will have no strange gods before him. If Christ, who is the Word Made Flesh, is one with the Father, that Father isn't Yahweh who is anything but the Incarnation of the Word. In the Book of Job if anyone is an Incarnation of the Word that is Love, it has to be Job himself. But the Old Testament Job is not free to recognize and proclaim his own divinity. Instead, he must defer to Yahweh to avoid the sin of pride that Adam and Eve committed as a result of their disobedient act in the Garden.

Yahweh, as the Father and The One True God, lacks compassion for Job's obedient suffering, and, as Jung indicates in his 'Answer to Job,' He displays his lack of wisdom when his son, Satan, is able to trick Him into thinking that Job is devious rather than obedient. A compassionate, wise and omniscient God could not be so tricked. He would feel secure in his own position and thus would be free from any fear of being surpassed by His children. Prostrating himself before such a Father may be a triumph for Job, but, still, such action guarantees the continued existence of that Father and the continued obedient suppression of individual potential. If Job is unable to accomplish the destruction of the Father, at least he should be able to recognize his own superiority to his Lord and Master. If the Master doesn't grant His servant equality, the Master himself is guilty of pride and thus lives in slavery to his own fear which, in turn, prevents him from acting with wisdom and compassion.

Reading the Book of Job, and the sacred scriptures themselves, as a record of "physical truth" is inadequate for our Age of Rational Science. Given the chaotic nature of our world—ushered in by the atomic explosion at Hiroshima in August of 1945—where there are "no more horizons," we, as Western individuals, should be free from the yoke of Yahweh. We aren't fee from it if we merely conclude that there is no God if Yahweh doesn't exist. If we conclude that God doesn't exist because Yahweh proves Himself to be unworthy of such a dignified and responsible title, we are, in Sartre's words, "doomed to be free." However, to accept such doom is not to live in freedom. On the contrary, it is to live in existential despair that only offers the hope of "waiting for Godot." And as we wait in our "Waste Land," we can contribute to the "Waste" by subscribing to the "mythological canons" associated with the likes of rock music and the shopping mall.

Moreover, we aren't free from the yoke of Yahweh, where we have no control over our own destiny, if we retreat into our churches whose pulpits continue to proclaim an obsolete reading of the sacred scriptures. Such a reading fails to acknowledge Christ, the Savior, as representing the transformation of Yahweh into the wise, omniscient Father He should have been all along. That Father would have set Job free in recognition of his equality with Him as an individual, living expression of the Word Made Flesh. When we read the sacred scriptures as an expression of "psychic truth," the Old Testament Father, Yahweh not transformed, cannot be the authentic Father to whom the individual owes obedience. The authentic Old Testament Father, to whom Christ refers and to whom the individual owes obedience, has to be the Serpent of Eden. Acting out of wisdom and compassion, the Serpent—free from fear and pride—encourages his children to eat the apple from the Tree of Knowledge to learn the secrets of good and evil and to "become as gods" like the Serpent himself. Only Yahweh transformed as Christ is free from fear and pride. And only Yahweh transformed as Christ is as "wise as a serpent" and as "harmless as a dove."

The psychological transformation of Yahweh into Christ is lost in a reading of the sacred scriptures that emphasizes their historical, "physical" truth as being their primary claim to validity. For the individual such a claim is valid only as long as their historical or "physical" truth remains unchallenged. As long as we don't question Christianity's claim to such truth, we can have faith in it as a "mythological canon" capable of gathering "toward a focus" our "energies of aspiration." However, when we begin, reasonably, to question its historical and "physical" claims, Christianity loses its efficacy as a "mythological canon." Knowingly or unknowingly, then, we can agree with Freud for whom it, as religion, should be replaced by science, and we can agree with Sartre for whom "everything indeed is permitted if God does not exist." Individual reason and the continuing impact of scientific discoveries combine to destroy the "affect power" of this "traditional" reading of Christianity, leading committed thinkers—such as Freud and Sartre—to conclude that Christianity itself is a lie. In effect, such a conclusion leaves us abandoned in a meaningless world where the extent of our aspirations, if we have any left, stops at sexual fulfillment, whether actual or sublimated through the acquisition of wealth—or both.

Considering the triumph of rational science and the power of human reasoning, Christianity has a chance to function as a "mythological canon" capable of gathering "toward a focus" our "energies of aspiration" only when we read it as an expression of Jung's "psychic truth." Only then does it possess the majesty to compete with the more immediate, and still emerging, "mythological canons" associated with the likes of rock music and the shopping mall. When we read it as an expression of "physical truth," amidst the wonders of rational science, Christianity presents the Hero in the person of Christ but reduces him to the status of an historical being in whom the responsible individual can take "no stock." Left without an authentic Hero around whom to gather "toward a focus" our "energies of aspiration," we can turn toward the immediate sexual and economic promise offered by the likes of rock music and the shopping mall. But by discovering the "psychic truth" inherent in Christianity, we still can answer Jung's 'Answer to Job.' In the process we can restore it to proper life—as a "mythological canon" capable of "gathering toward a focus" our "energies of aspiration."

When we read it psychologically, the transformation of Yahweh into Christ becomes a timeless expression of an individual's transformation from the state of the formative, infantile ego to that of the mature, adult ego. As timeless expressions of the infantile and adult egos, neither Yahweh nor Christ is dead. Rather, both are alive as mythic beings who, projected onto time, are free from it and therefore exist for all time. When we read them as mythic beings, both Yahweh and Christ are immortal and recognizable in the world of experience reflected in either the agrarian and nomadic Middle East of 2,000 years ago or in the industrial and scientific West of the 21st century and beyond. In any case, when it surfaces in the individual or nation of adult years, the infantile ego—and not nuclear power, for example—is the destructive force in the universe.

As an expression of its God's Kingdom on earth and hierarchically structured, both secularly and ecclesiastically, along the lines of its historical reading of Christianity, our Western world is in need of psychological transformation on both the individual and collective level. We can find the answer to the Sartrean lament of meaninglessness and despair, and thus to subsequent "mythological canons" associated with the likes of rock music and the shopping mall, in Jung's 'Answer to Job' and in the accompanying reading of Christianity as an expression of "psychic truth." Read as a work of art—as a "creative mythology"—Christianity is one of the "props" or "pillars" we need to help us "endure" and "prevail."

Yahweh had to become man to become God. In so doing, He set us free, as he set Job free, to become God ourselves.

When we read it as an expression of "psychic truth," Christianity not only allows each individual to live as God but also it expects each individual to live up to that responsibility. And the Serpent of Eden is the authentic Father to whom the God-Man Christ refers and to whom the individual owes obedience. The Serpent, as an authentic, mythological and archetypal Father, commands his children to "become as gods" like the Father himself. In this reading we sin and contribute to the destruction of life when we fail to obey the Father who, having taken the form of a serpent, knows no sexual distinction. If we avoid sin and obey the Father, we embark on the path that leads to the emergence of the mature, adult ego. We walk the Way of the Cross that ends in the alienated majesty of the crucifix only when the collective authority holds to the inadequate, obsolete reading of the "mythological canon" of Christianity. The transformation of authority from the infantile state of its Old Testament, Yahwistic expression to the adult state of its New Testament, Serpent manifestation makes the individual transformation that much easier.

Identified as the Father, parental authority—whether institutional or individual—should be an historical expression of the archetypal, Serpent authority. And because the Serpent is sexless, in opposition to the male Yahweh, the adult ego expressed in the Serpent isn't the sole domain of the male. In fact, males and females equally share the responsibility to follow the path of transformation from Yahweh to Christ, to walk the Way of the Cross. Only two individuals who walk that path can ever be equal in their necessary male and female opposition. And only the male and female individuals who walk that path of equality can experience the authentic love that is the Word that the individual, living as an expression of the adult ego, makes Flesh. The transformation of Yahweh into Christ indicates that the Incarnation is supposed to be accomplished in the very process of individual maturation, reinforcing the contention of Alan Watts whom Joseph Campbell quotes at the end of 'The Masks of God: Creative Mythology': "Thus the Incarnation is without effect or significance for human beings living today if it is mere history; it is a 'salvic truth' only if it is perennial, a revelation of a timeless event going on within man always."

A "creative" reading of the Christian Mythology, and of the Book of Job found in Jung's "answer," offers the revelation that the individual can live as God. The individual transformation from the state of the formative, infantile ego to that of the mature, adult ego results in the realization of individual freedom that, far from being our condemnation, proves to be our individual destiny instead. Moreover, the "creative" reading of Christianity and its Book of Job specifically promotes the equality of the opposite sexes with the authentic Father, to whom the individual owes obedience, being expressed in the form of a serpent rather than in that of a male or female personality to whose whims the individual is subjected. In effect, a "creative" reading of the Christian Mythology and its Book of Job supports Jung's idea of "reforms by retrogressions" where, in this case, the structuring mythology of a civilization, "instead of being wiped out," is "read symbolically for once." When we read it symbolically, the Christian Mythology offers the revelation that we, as individuals, are both the destroyers and creators of life on our planet.

When we find it evident in the infant, where it is natural, the formative, infantile ego is both necessary and harmless. However, as a "creative" reading of the Christian Mythology and its Book of Job illustrates, when we find that same ego in the person of adult years, its destructive capacity can threaten the harmony of our existence. In such circumstances the infantile ego is dominated by fear and pride, and most significantly of all, it is an ego devoid of authentic love that a curious reading of the "mythological canon" of Christianity celebrates as the creative power of the universe. This creative power of Love—celebrated as Amor in the poetry of the medieval troubadours as well as in the image of the crucified Christ—is expressed in the adult ego to which each responsible individual, male or female, aspires. When we read it "symbolically for once," the "mythological canon" of Christianity, with its Book of Job, has the "affect power" to gather "toward a focus" each responsible individual's "energies of aspiration" which transcend the level identified in Freudian psychology or in the "mythological canons" associated with the likes rock music and the shopping mall.

If we can "focus" our "energies of aspiration" on the adult ego, we also can free ourselves to live as creative manifestations of the Word Made Flesh. Thus authentic Love, celebrated in the poetry of the medieval troubadours and in the majesty of the crucifix, becomes a way of life in itself. To live Amor is to live the Way of the Cross which for Jung is to live the way that leads to the discovery of the "undiscovered self." And in his concluding paragraph of 'The Hero with a Thousand Faces,' published in 1949, Joseph Campbell emphasizes the individual challenge for now and the decades and centuries to follow:

> The modern hero, the modern individual, who dares to heed the call and seek the mansion of that presence with whom it is our destiny to be atoned, cannot, indeed must not, wait for his community to cast off its slough of fear, pride, rationalized avarice, and sanctified misunderstanding. 'Live,' Nietzsche says, 'as though the day were here.' It is not society that is to guide and save

the creative hero, but precisely the reverse. And so every one of us shares the supreme ordeal—carries the cross of the redeemer—not in the bright moments of his tribe's great victories, but in the silences of his personal despair.

"The modern hero, the modern individual...cannot, indeed must not wait for his community to slough off" its infantile ego. The community today is not just the tribe, the family or even the nation. Instead, it is the world itself that wouldn't be so visibly chaotic if it weren't dominated by the infantile ego still alive in its citizens of adult years. The world community, of which the West is a part, feels Campbell's "fear." It feels the psychological fear of time and death, if not that of nuclear destruction, and as Faulkner tells us, fear is the "basest of all things." Also, that same community lives the "pride" concretely expressed through Yahweh in the Book of Job and perpetuated, however innocently, by the institutional bigotry reflected in any Yahwistic institution. That same community lives the "rationalized avarice" identified by the omniscient Christ in the righteous Pharisee who loudly prays, dressed in all his finery, at the front of the temple. And that same community lives the "sanctified misunderstanding" that allows an archaic reading of the "mythological canon" of Christianity to be preached from pulpits in all corners of the Christian world.

Our Age of Rational Science calls for Heroes, and we can fulfill that role when we discover the way of life of Amor celebrated by the medieval troubadours and most emphatically in the agonized majesty of the Christian crucifix, living in support of a "creative," or "symbolic," reading of the Christian Mythology. Ultimately, the answer to Jung's 'Answer to Job' calls for the "modern hero," each "modern individual," to "dare to heed the call and seek the mansion of that presence with whom it is our destiny to be atoned"—in this case to be at-oned. The "modern individual," male or female without distinction or discrimination, as the "modern hero" carries it within his or her power to transform the world from a "community" identified with the destructive majesty of the infantile ego into one identified with the creative majesty of the adult ego. When we bring it to life, as we see expressed for us in Yahweh's transformation into Christ, the adult ego can restore order out of the chaos.

With the same spirit of building, creating and transforming that characterizes Jung's examination of the sacred scriptures of the Christian Mythology, the "modern individual"—the "modern hero"—can accept the responsibility to live as a Christ. Each of us can accept the responsibility to live as a Hero, as "an incarnation and revelation of God himself" in accord with Jung's "symbolic" understanding of the crucifix emphasized in 'The Undiscovered Self." Undoubtedly, "every one of us shares the supreme ordeal—carries the cross of the redeemer"—with courage and honor and pride and dignity and humility and pity and compassion and love not only "in the silence of his personal despair" but also "in the bright moments if his tribe's great victories."

10

The Nuclear Age: A Time for Heroes

When we acknowledge the scientific triumphs of the Nuclear Age, we no longer can live as if the original sin of Adam and Eve in the Garden of Eden were the rational cause for the existence of the monster that is life. In the face of this monster, which guarantees the death of every living member of our species, we need inspiration to help us "endure and prevail." If we assign the responsibility for providing the necessary heroes to sources other than ourselves, we still live as if the Garden of Eden story were a record of historical fact and as if eating the apple were the original sin of humankind that introduced death into the world. If we continue to live, amidst the discoveries of rational science, as though the Eden story provides us with the rational, historic cause for the undeniable effect of the "monstrous nature of life," we live without heroes and without the subsequent inspiration they provide. We live without the will to "endure" let alone "prevail." But if we accept and celebrate the scientific triumphs of the Nuclear Age and if we live with the recognition that Adam and Eve's story provides us with the necessary, life-supporting inspiration, we rediscover lost heroes. At the same time, we discover our own responsibility to live as hero.

The Garden of Eden story is the foundation of the Christian Mythology which, as we have seen, traditionally has enjoyed the status of being recognized as a record of historical fact. As long as that assigned historicity goes unchallenged, the Eden foundation and its accompanying mythology remains solid, providing the collection of individuals living under its influence with the structure that gives life a sense of stability and order. In "The Importance of Rites" from 'Myths to Live By' Joseph Campbell reminds us that "all life is structure," and, accordingly, "the more elaborate the structure, the more elaborate the life form." Given our elaborate structure, with mythology providing the building blocks, we—as individual expressions of humankind—represent the highest "life form." When the structuring principle of any group—whether tribe, family, nation or civilization—reinforces the empirical knowledge available to the individuals who compose the group, it has the power to create order and to grant individual lives a noble purpose that extends beyond India's "sheath of food." Before scientific discoveries so forcefully impacted Western life, the Christian Mythology, read primarily as a history, had the power to function as a living mythology. In the process it helped provide us with the heroes and the inspiration we needed to "endure and prevail."

However, with the emergence of the Nuclear Age we find ourselves without that inspiration. The scientific discoveries that have made our lives more comfortable than ever before also have shown us that the Garden of Eden story—and thus the mythology built on that once solid foundation—is not primarily a record of historic fact. Still subject to the influence of the discredited reading of our creation story and its accompanying mythology, we are left—at worst—with no sense of order, stability or inspiration. At best we are left with an obsolete sense of the same that no longer can provide the satisfaction associated with a living mythology. In effect then, as children of the Nuclear Age—that has seen the destruction of two Japanese cities and the landing of men on the moon—we have witnessed the spiritually affective death of our historically interpreted mythology. As a result, we can conclude that the death of this historic reading represents the final death of our mythology or, by default or even out of fear of there being nothing else, we cling to its obsolete reading. In either case we are left with little, or nothing, to live for but the "sheath of food" immediately visible to our eyes.

The mythological structure that traditionally supported Western life in its Christian era has crumbled only because its foundation, when we study it in the light of the Nuclear Age, doesn't stand up to the scrutiny. The scientific knowledge readily available to us doesn't reinforce any of its claims to historical and scientific accuracy. When we "look long," however, in that same light, neither the mythological structure of the West nor its foundation has been proven to be finally false. On the contrary, that same structure and that same foundation return to life supported, this time, by the very scientific knowledge that seemingly led to their deaths. None of us needs mythology to live, but we do need it to show us the way to live with a purpose that takes us beyond "the sheath of food." We do need mythology to show us the way to live as heroes—as individual, creative forces in our world. And if our Nuclear Age is a time for anything, it certainly is a time for heroes.

The Church, whether Catholic or Protestant, has tried to meet the challenge of the Nuclear Age by strengthening its ties to historicity because of a seemingly apparent conflict between science and religion where the discoveries of one—science—appear to negate the teachings of the other—religion. Therefore, the Church can see science as being the enemy of religion. However, when we "look long," through the eyes of the Nuclear Age, science plays anything but that role. In fact, only when we study it with eyes illuminated by scientific discoveries does religion begin to reveal its heroes and inspirational power. Science breathes fresh life into religion, enabling us to discover the psychological reading of our Garden of Eden story which then leads to the rebirth of the life-supporting mythology built on that foundation. The Christian Mythology, presented as a record of scientific and historic facts, may be dead forever. But that same mythology, presented as a record of experiential, psychological facts, has yet to be discovered.

The Christian Mythology and its creation story, like any authentic mythology, is born out of natural experience with life just as it is. Mythology expresses the truth of that experience, and if we read it primarily as a source of historic and scientific truth, we fail to discover its experiential truth. So, if we read Christianity and its creation myth scientifically, as an expression of psychological truth determined by experience with life, we read it for its natural, intended purpose. A mythology is a work of art, and no such work ever pretends to be primarily a record of historic and scientific fact. Instead, a work of art expresses the truth that anyone can experience, which accounts for the fact that various works from different environments in a variety of eras can present the same, fundamental conclusions. As a work of art the Christian Mythology is built on a foundation of conflict where the established authority seeks to keep the individual a child, thus retarding the natural process of maturation. When we read the mythology psychologically, through the eyes of the Nuclear Age, God—Yahweh—in the Garden of Eden story becomes a symbolic expression of an experienced authority proven to be more tyrannical and infantile than benevolent and adult.

The "adequate," heroic individual poses a threat to the existence of such an authority. As a result, God—Yahweh—does not want His children to eat the fruit from the Tree of Knowledge. Rather, He would prefer that they remain ignorant in order to preserve His own existence. Because it taught a non-experiential, historic reading of the Garden of Eden story, the Church assumed—and for all practical purposes continues to assume—the role of Yahweh. Therefore, as the Church of the authentic, Universal God of Creation, it expected obedience from its followers just as God expected obedience from Adam and Eve in their garden paradise. Solidly built on the virtue of obedience, that structure served Western civilization well into the 20th century, but it has crumbled with the emergence of the Nuclear Age. Scientific discoveries, more universally known than ever before, refute fundamental Church doctrine—most notably that of "mythic dissociation"—leaving us, as Western individuals, without the inspiration a living mythology can provide. We don't know whom or what we are supposed to obey to earn the salvation that allows us to transcend time and death—both of which remain a reality no matter how sophisticated the discoveries of rational science turn out to be. We can alter the conditions of the world with our science, but we cannot alter the conditions of life. We only can affirm the monstrous nature of life, in the manner of our primitive predecessors, and discover the secret of our otherwise meaningless existence where it's been expressed—undetected—all along.

By proving that death is natural, and not the result of any sin in any garden anywhere, science has freed us to discover and live our individual identity—to discover and live, finally, the mythological dimension of life that exists beyond the more immediate "sheath of food." As Western individuals, we are free, finally, to follow in the footsteps of our mythological parents—Adam and Eve—who, in disobedience to Yahweh, obediently answered the call of the Serpent and ate the fruit from the Tree of Knowledge. Before we felt the impact of science on the 20th and 21st centuries, we weren't free to follow in those footsteps because if we did, we would repeat the original sin of pride that, as we knew, destroyed the harmony of paradise. But now, living amidst the scientific progress that characterizes our Nuclear Age, we have learned that we misdirected our obedience. If we hadn't, we wouldn't find ourselves living in such a state of fragmented chaos. The Garden of Eden story still tells of the destructive force of pride, but its focus has shifted away from Adam and Eve, the traditional sinners in the Garden. Now all eyes have to be focused on Yahweh cast in the role of authority, of the Father, who doesn't grant His loyal subjects—His loyal children—equality, thereby upsetting the natural, experiential structure and order of human life.

In the Garden of Eden story, read through the eyes of our Nuclear Age, that natural, experiential structure is expressed in the Serpent—traditionally assigned the role of evil, in opposition to God, in the historical reading of the story. Given that traditional reading, it follows that individual obedience to the creative will of God should lead to the preservation of the established order of paradise, which, in fact, it does—but only at the expense of individual, psychological maturation. Also, as the emergence of our Nuclear Age can attest, that obedience leads to the continued dominance of authority—ecclesiastical or secular—as the protector of the individual, until pride overwhelms it or until its power becomes so mighty that if it were to be employed for the individual's protection, it could end up destroying that which it is supposed to protect. When either or both conditions are met, the once stable order and structure breaks down, resulting in chaos and confusion and leaving the established authority—stuck on its Yahwistic behavior—exposed as being unworthy of faith and trust.

In the face of this exposure we can discover the Serpent as the authentic God of Eden. As long as the order and structure created by the historical reading of the Christian Mythology remains intact, we have no need to discover any alternative reading. And none of us who have enjoyed the fruits of scientific discovery can deny the motivating influence of that structure and the heroes it at least appeared to help produce. However, that structure, built on a foundation that could not withstand scientific scrutiny, could not endure. If it's God's will that authority remain trapped in pre-scientific ignorance and if it's God's will that individuals remain trapped in the resulting obedience, there is little, or no, hope for any of us to "endure and prevail." In response to that despair, we can live lives "full of sound and fury signifying nothing," supported by the immediate glitter of the shopping mall or by the ultimate promise of the Christian pulpit—still standing on its traditional, but scientifically inadequate, premise of "mythic dissociation." By discovering the authentic God of Eden, we can redirect our obedience to the Serpent authority that commands us to eat the apple that leads to knowledge of good and evil. We are commanded to grow into omniscience, to achieve the maturational level of the adult ego, in the image of the authentic God. The new order that results from obedience to the will of the authentic God—the authentic Father—is based more on wisdom than on ignorance. Scientific discoveries, then, will only strengthen that order and individual faith in the God that supports it. When we read the Christian Mythology psychologically in our Nuclear Age, the Yahwistic authority proves itself to be infantile, unheroic and ultimately destructive. The Serpent authority, on the other hand, proves itself to be adult, heroic and immediately creative.

The maturation of the Western individual as hero has been delayed by obedience to the Yahwistic authority in an honorable attempt to avoid Adam and Eve's original sin of pride in the Garden. However, both the discoveries of rational science and the natural accumulation of experience with life have discredited the traditionally accepted historicity of that story, making it irresponsible to continue in that particular posture of obedience into the 21st century and beyond. By doing so, regardless of any noble, honorable intentions, we can—inadvertently if not intentionally—contribute more to the destruction of life than to its creation. Adopting a posture of disobedience, in reaction to our loss of faith in institutional authority, can lead to even more destruction because obedience is a prerequisite for love—the creative force which historically has united us at least within the boundaries of our diverse groups. Therefore, it's in our best interests, individually and collectively, to discover a level of obedience that extends beyond that commanded by the historical reading of the Christian Mythology. If there is no such level, we have no hope to take us beyond the promise offered by continued economic and technological progress.

When we read it psychologically, through eyes awakened by the accomplishments of our Nuclear Age, the seemingly irrelevant Garden of Eden story provides us with an understanding of obedience consistent with the scientific knowledge of the era. When we read that story as an expression of experiential—or psychological—truth, Yahweh, and all succeeding Yahwistic authority, regardless of intentions, proves to be unworthy of any individual's obedience. He, and any succeeding authority modeled in His image, governs more out of fear and pride than out of love and humility. Obedience remains a prerequisite for love and to love is heroic, but in our Nuclear Age to love and to live as hero in accord with Yahwistic Law, established as a result of Adam and Eve's original sin, can be destructively archaic. Our Nuclear Age has seen the end of the era of restrictive Yahwistic Law and demands that we, as Western individuals, discover the liberating Serpent Law—previously obscured by our obedient misreading of our creation myth.

When we read it psychologically, through the eyes of our Nuclear Age, the Garden of Eden story emerges more as a story of original obedience than it does as one of original disobedience. It becomes more of a timeless story of an individual decision to avoid sin than an historical account of Adam and Eve's decision to commit original sin. Remembering that "all life is structure" and remembering Jung's words telling us that "we cannot live the afternoon of life according to the program of life's morning," the Garden of Eden story, that still provides a solid foundation for individual and collective life within our Western world, waits to be read as a timeless story illuminating the path that avoids sin. In this reading, suitable for our Nuclear Age and beyond, Adam and Eve, as mythological—rather than historical—expressions of the first man and first woman, are faced with a conflict of obedience and not merely with the disastrous effects of disobedience. As mythological, rather than historical, expressions of the original man and the original woman, Adam and Eve are individual, local expressions of universal human, psychological potential for obedience and love, transcending any boundaries—or "horizons"—we may have erected over the years.

As mythological beings inhabiting their mythological Garden, Adam and Eve are faced with the conflict of having to decide to obey the established Garden authority, revealed in the person of Yahweh, or the still undeveloped, but awakened, natural authority of the "heart," revealed through the Serpent. Afflicted with fear and pride, Yahweh commands His children to avoid eating the apple from the Tree of Knowledge lest they become like Him which, were they to do so, would threaten His authority and very existence. On the other hand, the Serpent authority, being free from fear and pride, commands those same children to eat the fruit so as to know both good and evil and to be as he is—wise and omniscient. Adam, as the social individual mindful of his duty to obey social authority, is reticent, but Eve, as the natural individual drawn to her duty to obey natural authority, is not. Both Adam and Eve are equal in their capacity for obedience and love, but Eve is more willing to obey the Laws of Nature expressed through the Serpent who knows nothing about any historical Fall of Man. In the eyes of the natural, Serpent authority, eating the fruit from the Tree of Knowledge does not precipitate any fall from paradise. Rather, it leads to the affirmation of the "monstrous nature of life" and, through the quest for wisdom and omniscience, to the experience of paradise within it. The Yahwistic authority would have His children deny life, which has to include good and evil, and remain children. The Serpent authority would have those same children affirm that same life in order to remain "as children."

Unlike the male personality, Yahweh, the Serpent—as an expression of the universal power that constitutes the "heart" of the individual human being, Christian or otherwise—has no personality and no sex. The "heart" of the female is no different from that of the male, although the female isn't as preoccupied with any social identity. If anything then, this Serpent power is a feminine characteristic. By recognizing and obeying this natural power, all of us, male and female alike, can achieve our common destiny to live as hero, to live as God. We can live in wisdom, omniscience and in immortal affirmation of the nature of life that was then, is now and always will be both monstrous and noble. If the Serpent is God, the "heart" of the individual, the soul of the individual, the psyche of the individual is not naturally corrupt. The "heart" is only corrupt to the unnatural eyes of the Yahwistic authority whose vision is clouded by fear and pride, both of which prevent the realization of paradise that we are supposed to experience—individually and collectively—in life, here and now, just as it is. Eating the apple in order to know good and evil does not contribute to destruction. On the contrary, eating the apple to seek wisdom and to attain the omniscience that emerges as a result of natural experience can only contribute to creation.

When we read our creation myth as a story directing us to avoid sin, the Serpent, that lives as Jung's "psychic being," commands us to eat the apple and bring God to life. Such an understanding smacks of blasphemy only to the Yahwistic authority that may remain blind to the triumphs of human reason and its own rational science. In the context of our Nuclear Age no one can label, with any degree of certainty, the Serpent reading of the Garden of Eden story as being either blasphemous or heretical. But if we continue to embrace the doctrine of original sin, supported by the Yahwistic reading of the Eden story, we can only contribute—however inadvertently—to the psychological destruction of individual and collective life in our world. Throughout the history of the human race the need for hero never has been greater than it is in our contemporary era. As a result, we are challenged to live this life, here and now just as it is experienced, to meet that responsibility.

Building on experience and the conclusions associated with Joseph Campbell's work, the Garden of Eden story, read primarily as a "chronicle of fact," is part of a "traditional mythology" whose time has passed. Its history has been one of honor and glory, and by no stretch of the imagination should anyone condemn it as being evil. But that "traditional mythology," with its Yahwistic demand of obedience, did prevent the psychological maturation of the individual subject to its influence. Furthermore, the heroes that "traditional mythology" generated primarily were products of the Yahwistic authority structure itself, leaving us, as Western individuals, with the idea that hero was something separate from us and therefore beyond our reach. Within the Yahwistic structure of church or state we were "faceless" and had no control over our own destiny. In effect, we could experience no such thing as individuality. Those who proclaimed it, authentically or otherwise, were left to suffer the pains of various forms of excommunication, ranging from crucifixion, to burning at the stake and, finally, to isolated alienation.

We can discover authentic individuality, or authentic heroism, in the continuing Nuclear Age if we "look long" at the "creative" reading of our Christian Mythology that was then, remains now and always will be the structuring force in the life of our civilization. If the Christian Mythology isn't a "creative mythology" able to be experienced by any individual in any era, it is of no use beyond that of providing more material for dispassionate intellectual and academic analysis. If such is the case, we should then follow Freud's lead and see that it is replaced by science. But because the serpent power lives in every member of the species, we are creative mythologists at heart. If we can't give intellectual expression to our creations, we still can live them as artists with that designation being synonymous with individual and hero. Each individual, creative mythology, provided it emerges from honest eyes free from fear or pride or "rationalized avarice and sanctified misunderstanding," ultimately will reinforce the world mythology of Christianity. When we read it with those same "honest" eyes, the Christian Mythology then can reinforce James Joyce's "monomyth" that, in turn, assumes compatibility with the scientifically discovered—and experientially reasonable—"collective unconscious" associated with Carl Jung's mythologically inspired vision.

The crucifix, our fundamental, symbolic expression of the essence of Christianity, represents—for us—the most precise and clear revelation of the "collective unconscious" or "heart." When we see it in support of the Eden story read as an historical record of the disobedient Fall of Man, the crucifix gives New Testament expression to the Old Testament Yahwistic authority—more benevolent now but still separate from individual human beings and still having nothing to do with the Serpent authority of Eden. This reading yields no substantial difference between Old Testament and New Testament Law. God still is separate from us, and we see no transformation from Yahwistic Law to Serpent Law. We see the Church of the Son of God—Christ's Church—that becomes the Yahwistic authority the descendants of Adam and Eve have to obey if they hope to achieve union with the Father in His celestial paradise. However, when we see it in support of the Eden story read as a mythological record of the obedient Ascent of Man, the crucifix gives creative expression to the Serpent authority inherent in individuals—now fully mature and realized in the person of Christ crucified in agony only because the Yahwistic, Pharisaic authority hasn't attained his level of psychological maturation. When we "look long," with eyes made honest by the triumphs of the Nuclear Age, we can see that the crucifix represents authentic New Testament transformation from reliance on Yahwistic Law to acceptance of Serpent Law.

The authentic command of the New Testament, then, is the original command of the Serpent of Eden. Liberated finally and forever from the Old Testament command of Yahwistic Law, we are called to obey Serpent Law to ease the pain of the Savior and to live as God—to live as incarnations of the Word that is God and of the God that is Love. If God is Love and if God's Law is Love, that God and that Law have to be symbolically revealed in the Serpent who lives this inspired Law free from Yahwistic fear and pride. Serpent Law, as the fundamental Law of Nature, commands the individual—without mention of any Fall—to eat the apple and acquire knowledge of both good and evil. If we obey that Law, we eat the apple and experience life as it is, without any trace of original sin, in quest of the paradise we are supposed to experience here and now. If we obey Serpent Law as the fundamental Law of Nature, we embark on the Way of the Cross which is the way of natural—as opposed to Yahwistic—life. By following that path, we come to realize our own inherent heroism, previously obscured, and never consciously realized, as a result of our dutiful obedience to the imposed, unnatural Yahwistic Law.

Historically, we've lived in obedience to our Yahwistic authority that defines Love in terms of Agape. But Agape's charity demands no sacrifice of the magnitude and majesty expressed in the crucifix. Furthermore, if we accept Agape as representing the ultimate expression of Christian Love, we ignore the Serpent Law and glorify as heroes only those who are able to participate in the demonstration of Love that doesn't apply to the recipients of the charity. We certainly can't dismiss Agape as being unnecessary, but if we see it as the ultimate in Christian Love, we reduce it to a Love of convenience that has nothing to do with Serpent Law and Serpent Love whose crucified image lives in symbolic, agonized expression of the continued preservation of Yahwistic fear, pride and even ignorance. Unlike Yahwistic Law that doesn't release individuals to live their capacity for hero, Serpent Law commands the individual, male or female without distinction or discrimination, to allow the Hero—that is God—to live free from the agony of His crucified alienation.

When we read it through eyes made honest by the triumphs of the Nuclear Age, the Garden of Eden story reveals a more mature level of obedience, a more mature level of love and, ultimately, a more mature level of heroism. The story then commands individuals to live as incarnations of that Love in heroic obedience to Serpent Law that knows no distinction or discrimination. Moreover, the Serpent of Eden, expressed through the mature image of Christ, lives what it commands, thereby lending majesty to its presence. Also, as the Eden story attests, this Serpent power carries no specific sex, although it may emerge in any male or female "costume," which accounts for Christ's male identity. Therefore, claims of male superiority cannot emerge from the Serpent reading of the Garden of Eden story and its accompanying mythology. We can make those claims only when we read that story and its mythology through the eyes of the Yahwistic authority still holding fast to the traditional doctrine of "mythic dissociation." When we read it through the eyes of the Serpent authority, inspired by the scientific realities of the Nuclear Age, the Eden story, and its accompanying mythology, reveals a creative and unaccommodating affirmation of life as it is naturally experienced, without exception, by every member of the species.

When we "look long," in the light of Nuclear Age reality, the Garden of Eden story reveals a more mature level of obedience—obedience to the "heart"—a more mature level of Love—Amor or the naturally inspired Love identified in the Serpent—and a more mature level of heroism—the naturally, rather than institutionally, obedient individual as Hero. When we read it as a mythological account of the avoidance of sin, the Garden of Eden story chronicles the Ascent, rather than the Fall, of Man. As a result, the story commands the responsible individual to live the experience of that ascent to fulfill a natural, "mythic" duty that transcends any social duty we may find imposed upon us. The Serpent's evocative response eclipses Yahweh's coercive command. When we read the Garden of Eden story as a mythological account of the avoidance of sin, we take the initial, but maybe most important, step on Jung's road to "reforms by retrogressions." And taking that initial step can help any responsible individual discover Christ as the lost Hero of the Christian Mythology.

When we read it in support of the Garden of Eden story as a mythological account of the avoidance of sin, the succeeding story of Christ presents him as a concrete manifestation—as an incarnation—of the mature levels of obedience, love and heroism originally identified in the Serpent. When we see it as being free from any influence identified with the Yahwistic Fall of Man, Christ's crucifixion has nothing to do with sin. Instead, it has everything to do with the consequences that befall the responsible individual who, following the path of Amor, lives his or her potential in the face of a Yahwistic authority that hasn't experienced the necessary transformation that leads to the emergence of the Serpent authority. In terms of the principle of Love, Agape defines the Yahwistic authority while Amor does the same for the Serpent authority. If the Old Testament, Pharisaic authority were a Serpent authority, we would have no crucifixion. Similarly, if the succeeding Christian church authority were cast in the mold of the Serpent, we would have had few burnings at the stake during the Middle Ages, and we would have even fewer contemporary examples of unpublicized, isolated alienation. Ultimately, Christ, the lost Hero of the Christian Mythology, is crucified—alienated—because he lives as an expression of evocative Serpent Law—the at-one-ment Love of Amor—in respectful correction of imposed Yahwistic Law—the atonement Love of Agape.

Carl Jung reminds us, in "The Stages of Life," that "there is thinking in primordial images—in symbols that are older than historical man." The scientific realities of the Nuclear Age command us to discover, or rediscover, these "symbols" and the subsequent "primordial" thinking. Such thinking may not be rational, in accord with contemporary calculation, but if we deny its existence in the face of the modern world and the declining effectiveness—as well as affectiveness—of established Yahwistic authority, we contribute, however inadvertently, to the chaos that affects the order and stability of individual life. The Garden of Eden story, when we read it as a mythological account of the avoidance of sin, supported by the crucifixion of the lost Hero of the succeeding mythology, is an expression of such "primordial thinking." If we return to, or rediscover, such thinking as commanded by the scientific realities of our Nuclear Age, we can contribute to our psychological ascent and creation rather than to our psychological descent and destruction. If we live in obedience to archaic Yahwistic Law or in disobedient obedience to whatever seems comfortable and convenient, we live—no matter how inadvertently—for the destruction of the very life we are destined to create.

Dr. Jung further reminds us, in the same essay, that "these primordial images," or "symbols," are "ingrained in him (man) from the earliest times, and, eternally living, outlasting all generations, still make up the groundwork of the human psyche. It is only possible to live the fullest life when we are in harmony with those symbols; wisdom is a return to them." Jung's call to wisdom is the call of the Serpent for our century and the decades and centuries to come. To follow in the footsteps of our mythological parents, we have to heed the call to recapture, and then to continue with, the Ascent of Man. The "primordial" imagery of the Garden of Eden story and the "primordial" symbolism of the crucifix combine to express the soul of Jung's "modern man"—the modern individual, male or female without distinction or discrimination—has lost. If we read the formative Garden of Eden story as a mythological account of the avoidance of sin and if we rediscover the lost Hero of the mythology it supports, we discover—consciously, for the first time—the heroic potential of the individual human being. And that discovery frees all of us—forever—from any despairing resignation to a life "full of sound and fury signifying nothing" and restores to us our will to "endure and prevail."

11

Mythological Illiteracy: The Western World's Folly

The historical emergence of Western civilization has been, and continues to be, marked by innovation. Our world, past and present, is replete with scientific breakthroughs that have transformed our lifestyle from one geared to nature and the dependable movement of the sun to one geared to science and its seductive promise, through continued technological progress, of deliverance from our natural bondage. Never in the history of the human race has a collective civilization been so technologically literate. And conversely, never has that same collective civilization, celebrated for its technological literacy, been so mythologically illiterate. If all life is balance between pairs of opposites such as light and dark, life and death, rapture and anguish, Western civilization—and therefore its individuals—is dangerously out of balance with technology and mythology representing another pair of opposites. As we welcome the 21st century, technological literacy seemingly has become the Western world's fortune. But at the same time the accompanying mythological illiteracy certainly has become its folly.

Impressed with our Age of Rational Science and its collection of technological miracles, we have managed to associate mythology, in popular culture, with lie. Thus when we discover a particular thought or belief to be rationally false, we conclude that it's "just a myth." This popular attitude toward myth has far more serious consequences when it infects the Christian church, Protestant or Roman Catholic. By accepting, and even fostering, this attitude, such prestigious and influential institutions—no matter how inadvertently—contribute to our failure to acknowledge Christianity as being, essentially, a mythology. If we refer to Christianity as a mythology, in the face of our popular connotation of myth, we associate it with an expression of lies and not with an expression of the truth. Given this popular conception, Christianity has to be rationally, historically accurate to be considered true and believable. However, it's unreasonable to make such a claim in an age dominated by technological miracles, and it's even more unreasonable to insist on Christianity's historical accuracy and subsequent superiority to anything made up. When we consider Jung's mythologically inspired conclusion that "myth is more individual and expresses life more accurately than does science," we see that it is folly indeed to continue on such a path.

Because mythology is born out of individual experience with life just as it's supposed to be and always will be, world without end, we should not expect it to be, nor should we read it primarily as, a record of scientific and historic fact. As Joseph Campbell reminds us in 'The Masks of God: Creative Mythology,' myths are "poetic readings of the mystery of life from a certain interested point of view. But to read a poem as a chronicle of fact—to say the least—is to miss the point. To say a little more, it is to prove oneself a dolt." Traditionally, we have read our mythology as a "chronicle of fact," and the resulting mythological illiteracy has increased our dependency on rational science that never can deliver us from the monster that is life just as it always has been and always will be. As long as we think our mythology to be a record of lies at the very worst or an unsupported "chronicle of fact" at the very best, we remain ignorant of the very nature of life and, therefore, trapped in our own folly.

We act neither fairly nor honestly if we conclude that the traditional reading of the Christian Mythology, as a "chronicle of fact," always has been folly. A study of the Western world living under the influence of that interpretation reveals an experience with order and structure that our contemporary, post-Vatican II and post-moonwalk world cannot match. Because it was built on fear, however, the order and structure individuals experienced living under the influence of their "traditional mythology" had no chance of being permanent. Solidly built on the premise of "mythic dissociation," it stressed the fear of Hell, the subterranean next world to which unfaithful souls were condemned by their separate God who demanded, rather than commanded, their obedience.

This separate God rewarded the faithful souls, who obeyed His commands expressed through His Church, by admitting them into Heaven. In this celestial next world they could experience an eternity in the presence of the majestic beatific vision, forever denied their unfaithful counterparts whom God condemned to an eternity in the subterranean darkness of Hell. Even though we misinterpreted it to be historical and physical, experience with this mythological world had the power to both inspire and terrify any one of us as the glorious light of the Heavenly beatific vision provided a fitting contrast to the majestic darkness and horror of Hell. Even though the fear of that darkness and horror supported it, the belief did identify a noble purpose of life that looked beyond that offered by the more immediate social, technological and economic worlds. Built on the primarily historic reading of Christianity, this moral order and structure lent credence to the mythological dimension of life, which helps account for any contemporary sense of nostalgia for an irrevocable past and helps explain the archaic thinking that can accompany such longing.

Still, any experience with the moral order built on that traditional foundation of "mythic dissociation" proves to be invaluable because it clearly reveals the importance of a living mythology, even if fear of an eternity in Hell's subterranean darkness fuels that life. Living to experience Heaven, motivated by fear or inspired by love, certainly proves to be more noble than living only for immediate rewards as if they, and nothing else, define life. To hold the ideas of Heaven and Hell in serious regard creates—at the very least—the appearance of nobility that in turn creates—also at the very least—the appearance of an immediate, physical world alive with inspiration. This essentially medieval structure, built around belief in a celestial Kingdom of Heaven and a subterranean Kingdom of Hell, worked its magic well into the 20th century. Anyone fortunate enough to have lived with its subsequent moral order had the chance to learn that we experience authentic life only when we follow the dictates of a living mythology.

That moral order, experienced by all pre-Vatican II and pre-moonwalk generations, has broken down as we enter the 21st century. The fear that supported the order has dissipated. We have experientially explored our celestial terrain and have found no evidence to support the physical existence of the Kingdom that, in the days of the traditional moral order and structure, housed the souls of the faithful departed. With the existence of this celestial Heaven discredited as a result of our inevitable, experiential exploration, we are free from our fear of the subterranean Kingdom of Hell. Manned celestial exploration has reinforced our own developing reason, and any remaining belief in the celestial and subterranean Kingdoms of Heaven and Hell lacks the conviction that characterized the days before we ventured out into our celestial terrain. The collective Western world, since the triumph of Augustinian argument in the fifth century, never has been mythologically literate, but the illiteracy that, ironically, served as its fortune in the days before celestial exploration now serves as its folly instead. In the wake of our courageous celestial adventure, we either unconvincingly retreat into our irrevocable past, idealistically look toward the future or despairingly live in the present as if there were "no more to life than death."

That the institutional church, holding fast to its doctrine of "mythic dissociation," continues to function in the Age of Rational Science provides ample proof that the past, no matter how irrevocable, still holds solid, nostalgic appeal. But no matter how impressive its numbers may be, any retreat remains unconvincing because the doctrine of the separation of God and His creations, calculated on the historical premise of original sin, no longer rings true in the face of developing human reason and its accompanying scientific adventures—led by our manned exploration of this separate God's celestial terrain. Moreover, by retreating into the past and defending the essence of traditional doctrine, we can, in the process, reduce the Church's stature to a level more compatible with that of a social club. Individuals, the "iron" in Chaucer's medieval metaphor, deserve better from the institutional "gold" to complete his alchemical image. If the "gold" rusts, the "iron" follows suit through their social identification. The alchemical image of turning base metal into gold then breaks down completely.

If we must live with a separation between the institution and the individual, the "gold" and the "iron," the institution should act in the best interests of the individual just as the shepherd should act in the best interests of his flock. If for some reason the shepherd acts in his own self interest instead, he does so at the expense of his flock. But if the sheep are at the mercy of the shepherd, individuals are not at the mercy of the institution. Furthermore, our experience with institutional authority during the long course of our historical emergence on our planet proves that authority, no matter how inadvertently, can deceive. If the Church could free itself from economic concerns and from the intellectual restraints associated with its traditional doctrine of original sin, it could confront the discoveries of rational science with wonder and awe in the spirit of continued growth and maturation. It could recognize the compatibility of the two seemingly contrary forces of science and religion and seek to preserve, or may even to create for the first time, the necessary balance between the opposites of technology and mythology. It could recognize that if science necessarily contributes to our comfort, religion, included in the world of mythology, certainly contributes to our satisfaction. Without that life-supporting balance we can live in a spiritual waste land of deceiving oases that, no matter how unconsciously, offer us only social clubs masquerading as churches.

With a history of obedience to the dictates of authority, the sheep can flock to the shepherd who then can deceive, no matter how unintentionally, because without a flock to tend the shepherd has no identity or reason to exist. When we see it metaphorically, as a shepherd tending to its flock and understandably fearing the scientific threat to traditional doctrine, the institutional church—Protestant or Catholic—can lead the retreat into the irrevocable past. If so, it then becomes the bastion of archaic, rather than creative, thought, leaving its flock of traditionally obedient sheep without the spiritual satisfaction and direction they expect the shepherd to provide. By retreating into obsolescence we can make a lie out of that which once was true, in keeping with Jung's discovery that "we cannot live the afternoon of life by the program of life's morning." The pulpit message of love, calculated on the archaic premise of "mythic dissociation" and original sin—supported by traditional hymn singing and reformed altar celebration—no longer generates authentic "affect power." As a result, the individual believer, as opposed to the mere pretender, is left to wonder where the magic of the past has gone.

In the absence of our hymnal or altar magic, we can continue to flock to our churches—now only masquerading as such—or we can disdain the masquerade, celebrate our liberation and turn our attention, primarily, to science and its continually innovative, technological miracles. In each case we face an idealistic image of a future structured around Christian love, the charitable Agape as preached from the pulpit, or structured around scientific promise—the technological paradise that replaces the now foolish, discredited mythological paradise that once served as the inspiration for religious thought and aspiration. Ironically, this idealism offers the image of a wedding between religion and science in that the church's pulpit Agape supports the promise of a technologically delivered paradise. However, such promise, supported by Agape and born out of mythological illiteracy, cannot claim any basis in authentic experience. Therefore, in spite of any immediate attraction, ultimately it is doomed and destined to lead to disillusionment—oftentimes loudly displayed in the pride and despair reflected in the frenzied multitudes who "can't get no satisfaction."

The Rolling Stones' 1965 hit song, 'Satisfaction,' provides a suitable anthem for the post-Vatican II and post-moonwalk Western world that, in the absence of its traditional order and structure, can live in a moral and spiritual waste land masked by the glitter of its technological miracles. As Faulkner might say, referring to his Nobel Prize address, we live more "of the glands" than we do "of the heart." Before the epochal events of Vatican II and the 1969 moonwalk, and in the absence of credible, experiential evidence to the contrary, we held the mythological concepts of Heaven and Hell in higher regard. Consequently, we saw a noble purpose to life that took us beyond the immediate "sheath of food" that only can satisfy the "glands." But if we once lived more to satisfy the "heart," the fear of punishment for living otherwise had to supply much of our motivation. Now that the experiential discoveries of our celestial explorers have eliminated our fear of the separate God's subterranean "prison house," we can take as much delight in disparaging the mythology that created the previous moral order and structure as we do in searching for an understanding of it that would be consistent with our accumulated, experiential evidence. The Old Testament, Yahwistic "Grand Design" of the Western world has crumbled. As a result, we wander in the chaos of our mythological illiteracy, oftentimes overcome by despair and self-pity—made even more depressing by the loss of wonder that accompanies the demise of a mythology that gives eloquent expression to both the mystery of life and the subsequent majesty of the individual.

But we don't have to wander aimlessly in our illiterate darkness. Instead, we can redirect our commitment to obedience to focus, not on the dictates of authority, but on the dictates of experience instead. Free from the bondage of fear and not limited to a life of indiscriminate Agape favored by the Christian pulpit, we can obey the discriminate Amor once awakened, unconsciously, by hymnal and altar magic. Fulfilling one aspect of this noble purpose, we can direct our individual love of devotion and commitment, once reserved solely for Christ as the earthly, historical expression of the celestial God, toward an immediate, worthy individual—as determined by the eyes and the heart. We can replace the crumbled, Old Testament "Grand Design," built on "mythic dissociation," with a fresh, New Testament "Design," built on "mythic association." In the process we can elevate the inspired, experiential love of Amor to the level of the Godhead where it always has belonged. In effect, the wondrous discoveries associated with the continuing exploration of our celestial terrain have vindicated the fifth-century Pelagian heresy. In Pelagius' view individuals have no need for "supernatural grace" because we, ourselves, are full of "natural grace." An institution holding views that run contrary to accumulated, experiential evidence can assume heretical status as we journey into the 21st century and beyond.

In the face of any such institutional heresy, we can discover that our commitment to obedience, regardless of the supporting motivation, created the now nostalgic moral order and structure that necessarily supports authentic life. Even if the order created by that Old Testament obedience has crumbled, we haven't lost our identity with that virtue as a result. We can discover that creative source of our nobility and direct it toward authentic experience that once, before the development of institutional authority, furnished us with our primary authority. If the institutional church is ever again to play a creative role in the life of the Western individual, it has to acknowledge its past history of "doltish" behavior, recognize the danger of continuing on that same path and discover its Christian Mythology as "a poetic reading of the mystery of life from a certain interested point of view." By discovering the magic of this "poetic reading of the mystery of life," the Church could help restore integrity—or perhaps create it for the first time—to Chaucer's 14th century alchemical image of the "gold" and "iron."

But we aren't without recourse if institutional reform leaves us to our own devices. Because we retain our capacity for obedience, regardless of any worldly conditions, we can recognize the value of that virtue and realize that we don't have to live in slavery to any popular voice to which we assign the role of authority. If we are responsibly interested in obedience, following the path of the Hero in any one of a "thousand faces," our experience with the "monstrous nature of life" still can awaken our "heart." We then can follow that "heart" to walk the path of the Hero celebrated in mythology that offers a "poetic reading of the mystery that is life." Such a living mythology affords all of us the opportunity to follow its direction, reinforcing that indicated by our own accumulated experience with the "monstrous nature of life." If the mythology of authority, reflected in the traditional, orthodox teaching of the institutional church, is coercive, the mythology of experience, reflected in the "great pagan mythologies" and in the "poetic" reading of the Christian Mythology, is evocative. Nonetheless, that coercive era of mythological illiteracy, mistaken for mythological literacy, is part of our heritage. We should remember it more for its life-supporting moral order, created by individual obedience to authority, than for its life-destroying social chaos, created by internal squabbles whose perpetuation ultimately led to the production and explosion of the atomic bomb.

By discovering our noble capacity for obedience and by directing it toward experience, we can achieve individual mythological literacy within a collective civilization that may—out of fear, pride or ignorance—remain mythologically illiterate. If we can discover this noble capacity and direct it toward experience—"the path directly before one, of the eyes and their message to the heart"—we then can follow the experiential path of "integrity and truth." Ironically, by discovering our noble capacity for obedience and by directing it toward the path of experience, we rediscover the ancient, "archetypal" path revealed in "the great pagan mythologies" where there is "emphasized throughout an essential reliance on nature." William Wordsworth echoed his support for this "essential reliance" in his 19th century poem 'The Tables Turned' when he instructed us to "come forth into the light of things" and "let Nature be your teacher." Obedience to Wordsworth's experience with "Nature" brings us into the "light of things," rendering us mythologically literate and free.

Continuing with the irony, the contemporary individual who "comes forth into the light of things" rediscovers the path illuminated by "the great pagan mythologies" originally disparaged by the institutional church for their lack of historical validity. In the eyes of the emerging Christian authority "the great pagan mythologies" already in existence were lies to be replaced by the One

Revealed Truth that church authority held in its possession. Thus the subsequent imposition of the authoritative, rather than experiential, or "poetic," reading of the Christian Mythology, gave birth to the popular conception that associates mythology with lie—and successfully delayed the psychological maturation of the Western world. Consequently, as we progress into the 21st century and beyond, we face a crisis of faith the proportion of which we have never experienced in our illustrious history. We can continue to wander in the darkness of our folly or we can "come forth into the light of things" and "let Nature by our (your) teacher."

In our Age of Rational Science we do have Carl Jung's mythologically inspired discoveries, especially the science of "individuation," to help lead us out of the darkness and into "the light of things." Related to the inquiring, classical Greek thought of antiquity, "individuation" stresses a world of light that revolves around the individual. As such, it represents more than another intellectual concept suitable only for academic discussion. Instead, it is an experiential idea to which Jung gave an intellectual name. "Individuation" is an experiential idea expressed in "the great pagan mythologies" where the Hero "as though moved by an infallible natural grace, follows without fear the urges of his heart." Such a mythological Hero does not follow, out of fear of punishment, the "urges" of any institutional church. Because his path is one inspired by experience and not dictated by authority, it parallels Jung's maturational path that leads to authentic life and to the realization of individual, psychological potential. If we can follow this path of light, out of obedience to Wordsworth's "Nature," we can restore "integrity and truth" to the moral and spiritual "Waste Land" that metaphorically defines the state of our mythologically illiterate Western world.

It is understandable to debate Jung's "scientific rediscovery of ancient wisdom," which includes his science of "individuation," amidst the order and structure that characterized 19th and 20th century life—until we felt the effects of Vatican II's altar reform and our triumphant walk on the surface of the moon. Jung's "scientific rediscovery" included the rediscovery of the God, the "psychic being," inherent in—rather than separate from—the individual. Such an idea has to be threatening, and seemingly heretical, in the absence of any empirical evidence to support it. Without such evidence, and given the popular attitude toward the mythology that inspired Jung's thought in the first place, we can hardly expect anyone to heed his "scientific rediscovery." However, such doubts, that once seemed reasonable in the years preceding Vatican II and the moonwalk, now can seem unreasonable—and even destructive—in the years following those epochal events.

As Joseph Campbell reminds us, it's "not authority but aspiration" that "is the motivator, builder, and transformer of civilizations." With our Old Testament "Grand Design," built around "mythic dissociation," discredited by the very scientific discoveries it helped inspire, the era of authority as the "motivator" and "builder" is over. But the end of the era of authority—marked by its mythological illiteracy—doesn't have to result in relegating the individual to the role of an aimless wanderer in a waste land dependent on the seductive, but deceptive, promise its technological miracles have to offer. We, as Western individuals, have a history of obedience. If we can rediscover that legacy and redirect it from authority to experience, we can rediscover the path of the Hero celebrated in the previously discredited "great pagan mythologies." Jung scientifically rediscovered that path of "individuation"—the path further illuminated by the individuated Christ crucified on his Cross of Wisdom.

Christ remains primarily historical, and therefore superior to the Heroes of "the great pagan mythologies," only in the eyes of the uninspired, or in any eyes governed by fear, pride or ignorance. But if we "look long," with the eyes of inspired experience governed by humility and insight, we can see the mythological Christ who is equivalent to, and as useful as, those same Heroes. Christ's history actually is a "poetic reading of the mystery of life from a certain interested point of view." His history actually is a mythology that we previously have read as "a chronicle of fact" in the manner of a "dolt." Consciously or unconsciously, the Christian authority, the "gold," played that role for the "iron" who then, in their subsequent obedience and social identification, unconsciously lived as "dolts." The "doltish" reading of the Christian Mythology discouraged the natural process of "individuation," leaving someone like Carl Jung with the opportunity to scientifically rediscover it when the time was ripe. When we study it in light of Jung's discovery, the crucifix symbolically portrays the "individuated" Hero crucified in agony only because institutional authority itself, demanding obedience to its dictates, has not—unlike the crucified Hero—"come into the light of things." To such an authority, stuck on its doctrine of a separate, celestial God, "Nature" is the realm of darkness and, therefore, has nothing of salvatory value to teach.

As long as we continue to insist on the existence of that separate God, in light of scientific and experiential evidence to the contrary, as being the last word on the subject, we will remain trapped in the darkness of our mythological illiteracy. As a result, we run the risk of guaranteeing the permanent spiritual death of a collective civilization, only delayed from reaching its destiny as a collection of "individuated" heroes descended from the "great pagan mythologies" of its antiquity.

As long as we insist on the existence of that separate God as being the last word, we preserve an Old Testament "Grand Design" already laid to rest by a New Testament vision. When we read it "poetically," this fresh "Grand Design" emerges as an experiential mythology—in accord with "the great pagan mythologies"—that encourages the natural process of psychological maturation Jung rediscovered and labeled "individuation." A creative civilization, moved by "aspiration" to "motivate," to "build" and to "transform," fosters and encourages this "individuation" process. It is a civilization willing "to come forth into the light of things" to let "Nature" be its "teacher," enabling it to emerge out of the darkness and folly of its mythological illiteracy and into the light and fortune of its mythological literacy. The symbol of the crucifix, that supported Christianity's traditional, and illiterate, atonement premise can and does support its creative, and literate, at-one-ment premise, placing it in accord with the experiential wisdom of "the great pagan mythologies" that poetically and magically revealed the "mystery of life" to any obedient heart.

The history of our Western world tells us that we, its individuals, possess that heart, and we have the crucified image of the Hero in the "face" of Christ to show us the proper path to follow. When we see Christianity as "a poetic reading of the mystery of life from a certain interested point of view," the path of the crucifix reinforces the already illuminated pagan path of an "essential reliance on nature" where the Hero "as though moved by an infallible <u>natural</u> grace, follows without fear the urges of his heart." The alienation of the Hero, symbolized in the crucifix, decreases in direct proportion to the number of individuals who—when awakened to their noble capacity for obedience—choose to obey the "urges of the heart." Obedience to the inspired path of experience represents the most psychologically mature level of obedience we can attain. If God is Love and if Christ is the New Testament, Christian expression of the Universal God, by following Christ—by following the Hero along that noble path—we live as incarnations of God. Such incarnations then "communicate to a life" not just "integrity and truth" but most importantly "the radiance of eternal life."

Rediscovering the lost path of experience, the path of mythological literacy, remains the primary innovative task facing our post-Vatican II and post-moonwalk era. If we can rediscover, and subsequently live, that path, we can work toward the creation of a New Order, toward the creation of a New Testament "Grand Design" supported, and even strengthened, by the discoveries of rational science and by those of our continuing exploration of our previously inaccessible celestial terrain. This authentic and indestructible "Grand Design," inspired by experience, celebrates a world of light that sees "individuated" human beings shining brightly on center stage. If we can "come forth into the light of things" and let "Nature be our (your) teacher," we can take a "giant leap" toward creating the proper, life-supporting balance between the opposites of technology and mythology. Alive with the inspired promise of mythological literacy, we then can ensure the continuing fortune of the Western world.

12

At the Crossroads: The Crucifix or the Golden Arch

When we think of Western civilization, we readily think of progress and innovation, and—at least in the 20th century, and now the 21st—we most closely associate our own country with that progressive and innovative spirit. America developed and exploded the atomic bomb, for example, and landed the first man on the moon. Harnessing the power of the atom and landing men on the moon represent triumphs not just for America but for the Western world itself being free to pursue the path of scientific inquiry and discovery. However, the dawn of the 21st century has witnessed the subsiding of the prevailing spirit that accompanied the adventurous path of scientific exploration and innovation. The triumph of the first atomic blast quickly gave way to the fear that followed, and the euphoria that greeted human beings' first walk on the moon has given way to indifference. As a result, the minds of immediate youth, as well as those of forgetful adults, associate America more closely with shopping malls and fast food outlets than with atomic and space age triumphs. We shouldn't be surprised then, as we enter the 21st century, to see McDonalds' Golden Arch emerge as perhaps the most popular identifying symbol of America—the country that led the human race to the moon.

Such a phenomenon would be of little or no concern if symbols themselves carried little or no consequence. However, in spite of any rational protestations to the contrary—resulting from our reliance on, and faith in, the language of words—symbols and their accompanying language can play a vital role in the development, and identification, of cultures and civilizations. In popular American lore, for example, the white man—when we see him, metaphorically, as an expression of the rational man of words—often speaks with "forked tongue" while the red man—when we see him, metaphorically, as an expression of the natural man of symbols—recognizes the deception. Only when the white man's rational language of words reinforces the red man's experiential language of symbols does the Native American deem him worthy of his association. Thus in America's popular 'Legend of the Lone Ranger' Tonto, the inarticulate, natural man, christens the Lone Ranger, the articulate, rational white man, as "kemo sabe" or "faithful friend." If the Lone Ranger were a rational man of deception, he would prove himself unworthy of Tonto who, while playing the role of natural man ignorant of the rational language of words, remains well-schooled in the experiential language of symbols. And as Joseph Campbell reminds us, that quiet, magical language works "through the eyes to the listening heart."

As the Lone Ranger's faithful companion would understand, the foundation of any culture or civilization is not economic, no matter how much the worldwide proliferation of McDonald's Golden Arch suggests otherwise. Antithetical to any experiential understanding, the Golden Arch celebrates economics—specifically capitalist economics—as representing the triumphant and solid foundation of Western civilization. Tonto, however, provided we still see him as a metaphor for the natural, experiential individual, would recognize—before the advent and need for rational, economic systems—that the foundation for human life, and the culture supporting it, more properly is mythological. Because his experience would prove that there would be no life without the sun, Tonto, our metaphorical expression of the natural individual, would see that constant and visible power as a fitting symbol on which to build an emerging culture. Thus natural, pagan religion, regardless of its "costume," would pay tribute to the Lord and Giver of Life in the form of sun worship. Any necessary, economic transactions then would be conducted within this essential, religious—or mythological—framework.

Such a framework gives structure to life within its cultural boundaries and provides a proper atmosphere for conducting rational, business and economic affairs as long as the structure itself remains believable. However, when that formative, mythological structure loses its credibility—for whatever reason—life once lived within and in support of it is left with only its economic dimension. The mythological dimension to that life effectively dies only remaining, if it does so at all, as an obsolete reminder of the majesty that was. Under such conditions we are left to conduct life within the resulting "Waste Land," easily masked by the affluent glitter of its apparent economic success. In our spiritual desert any symbolic expression of the once living mythological dimension loses its "affect power" and dies, leaving any individual, "listening heart" only with more immediate, economic symbols to "gather his energies" to "a focus."

Having reached the end of its Mythological Age, the culture can elevate the remaining economic dimension to the level of mythology and religion in response, thereby replacing any mythological expression of the Godhead with a corresponding economic expression. In effect, it can render "unto God" something that necessarily belongs to "Caesar." The Western world has the crucifix as its mythological counterpart to economics' Golden Arch, but when we see it in light of the scientific discoveries that have accompanied our economic success, neither the crucifix nor the mythology it supports is believable. A mythology based on an historical original sin committed in an historical garden cannot live and speak to any potential "listening heart" in an age that has proven its institutional claims to scientific and historical accuracy to be in error. Without an actual sin in any garden, we have no need for the redemption for that sin. If we have no need for such redemption, we have no need for the crucifix. We then are left to celebrate the glories and promise of our more immediate and seductive economic symbols—such as McDonald's, or America's, Golden Arch.

Individual human beings have to possess a dual, rather than singular, nature. If not, we would see no evidence of the existence of any mythological dimension to life that speaks to something other than the comfort of our physical nature. With numerous Christian churches prominently celebrating either the crucified or risen Christ in the crucifix or the barren cross, the Western world abounds with evidence that supports its recognition of life's mythological dimension. The image of the crucified Christ, more than that of the risen Christ, supports the essence of the Christian Mythology because traditional, orthodox teaching tells us that the suffering and death of the Savior atones for sin. However, the discoveries of rational science refute that teaching and deny the historicity of the Garden of Eden story, thus eliminating our need for redemption from sin as well. Without any need for that redemption, we are free to celebrate and worship at the shrine of the Golden Arch. In the process, however, we allow our triumphant scientific discoveries to deprive us of our chance to live with our economic accomplishments but for our mythological promise. So, we have reached a pivotal crossroads in our continuing adventure with the "monstrous nature of life." We can devote ourselves to economic immediacy, symbolized by the likes of the Golden Arch, or we can resurrect the crucifix and properly "render unto God the things that are God's and unto Caesar the things that are Caesar's." If we can achieve that balance, we can breathe fresh life into the "Waste Land."

Without its mythological dimension life cannot be truly human because only the human mind can function on this psychological level—the level of the "second mind." Furthermore, only the human mind needs to function on this level, as well as on that of the economic, "first mind." Only the human mind can comprehend the mystery of death and, therefore, the mystery of life. When we see it in this light, the triumph of the Golden Arch takes on greater significance. It reflects a gradual shift in emphasis in Western civilization first away from its formative, experiential foundation—expressed in the natural symbol of the sun—to its more recent institutional foundation—expressed in the orthodox reading of the crucifix—and, finally, to its current economic foundation—expressed in the economic symbol of the ubiquitous Golden Arch. By elevating the Golden Arch—capitalist economics—to the level of mythology and religion, whether consciously or unconsciously, we have rendered "unto God" something that necessarily belongs to "Caesar." In the process we have robbed human life of its sense of mystery and awe, resulting in the creation of the "Waste Land" masked by the glitter of our economically oriented progress.

We can take the first step toward discovering the way out of this desert by courageously recognizing the seductive nature of its economic glitter. The imposition of the institutional, non-experiential premise of original sin—coupled with the inevitable emergence of rational science and its triumphant discoveries—made the creation of our "Waste Land" predictable. If those scientific discoveries had supported institutional claims concerning original sin and the mythology built upon it, we could have avoided this desert condition. But if we "look long" with honest eyes, we can see that such is not, and has not, been the case. A mythological message, intended for the "second mind," that is refuted by the discoveries of rational science is of no affective use in that world because the refuted message is unreasonable. However, a mythological message, intended for that same mind, that is reinforced by those discoveries is of such use because the supported message is reasonable. As long as we find the courage to acknowledge it and our responsibility for its creation, and if we embrace the proper, reasonable reading of our mythological message, we can discover the way out of our contemporary "Waste Land."

The crucifix, rather than the barren cross, remains the symbolic essence of that mythological message. But when we read it reasonably, in full view and acceptance of the discoveries of rational science, we learn that it has nothing to do with original sin. For that doctrine to be true, enabling its crucifix to generate the subsequent "affect power" to provide direction for an individual's life, the Garden of Eden story has to be scientifically and historically accurate. A mythological message intended for the "second mind," based on the historic and scientific accuracy of that story, generated that power only in the absence of any readily available scientific evidence that could refute the institutionally authorized interpretation of the Eden events. However, the presence of such evidence renders that same message impotent. Furthermore, any "dream" offered as an extension of that mythological message emphasizing the primacy of the institutional structure experiences that same fate. By its very nature, such a dream—focusing on institutional responsibility at the expense of individual maturation—has to be either legislatively or economically based. Thus it requires little, if any, authentic sacrifice from the individual—male and female without distinction or discrimination.

Mythology necessarily is the "stuff" of dreams, but those projections onto the world of time are not, and never can be, directed to the legislative and economic worlds. Rather than referring to events belonging to the historical realm of the "first mind," such dreams refer, instead, to events belonging to the psychological realm of the "second mind." Therefore, a noble dream that speaks primarily to legislative or social, economic action—the historical realm of the "first mind" to which the institutional mythology of the crucifix speaks as well—lacks sufficient depth to awaken the "second mind" where the sense of individual responsibility and sacrifice resides. The dreamers of the "first mind," then, are not "archetypal" in nature. An "archetypal" dreamer seeks to awaken the individual's "second mind"—the mind that, when awakened, makes us properly "human." When we see it as supporting the institutional doctrine of original sin, the crucifix refers to events occurring in the historical realm of the "first mind." Such an interpretation holds little, if any, regard for individual creativity that resides in our properly "human" "second mind."

However, when we see it in a fresh light, free from the visionary constraints of original sin, the crucifix refers to events that occur in the psychological realm of the "second mind." In this reading the crucified Savior symbolically represents individual human beings and their capacity to dream. And that Savior, any "archetypal" dreamer, is crucified—alienated—because his "great expectations" exceed those of the crucifying—alienating—institutional authority and accompanying social order. That institutionally supported order disregards the psychological realm of human experience, or any "second mind," and embraces only the social, historical realm of the "first mind." But only when we acknowledge and affirm the "monstrous nature of life," that has to include death, do we awaken to the reality of the "second mind" and render ourselves properly "human." The "great expectations" of the "archetypal" dreamer, then, extend beyond the bounded realm of historical experience—in which events occur only once in time—to the boundless world of psychological experience—in which events constantly occur and reoccur actually free from time. Thus the crucifix is profoundly linked to the sun as a natural symbol and just as profoundly severed from the Golden Arch as a purely capitalist, economic symbol.

Any social order, for whatever reason, that lives more in accord with the path of the Golden Arch, rather than with that of the crucifix, necessarily places its emphasis on legislative and economic action. As a result, its dreamers speak only to the historical realm of the "first mind" in direct opposition to the "archetypal" dreamers who speak to the psychological realm of the "second mind." Dreams and dreamers limited to the historical realm of the "first mind" are idealistic and ultimately doomed because they focus their energy on the sacrificial potential of institutional authority. On the other hand, dreams and dreamers committed to the psychological realm of the "second mind" are romantic and ultimately destined because they focus their energy on the sacrificial potential of individual human beings. If institutions welcome them, dreamers of the "second mind" render those institutions affective because the individual represents the soul of the institution in the first place. The institution does not represent the soul of the individual. The "archetypal" dreamer, manifested in the natural, experiential symbol of the crucifix, for example, does not surrender his or her soul to the institution. Instead, such dreamers attempt to awaken the soul of their fellow individuals so that they may, in turn, create the soul of the institution.

If ever a country were founded on a dream and if ever a country prided itself on its sense of individuality and freedom, that country has to be America. And if America's melting pot of individuals lives primarily to experience the immediate, economic promise symbolically reflected in McDonald's Golden Arch, it lives contrary to the American Dream. That dream revolves around aspirations not limited to the level of the "first mind." As a result, the authentic American Dream finds more support in a natural, mythological symbol such as the crucifix than it does in an unnatural, economic symbol such as the Golden Arch. The crucifix, viewed as an evocative, experiential symbol—rather than as an imposed, institutional symbol—does not belong exclusively to the Roman Catholic Church and its particular institutional interpretation of the Christian Mythology. Instead, it belongs to individuals as an example of a universal, "archetypal" symbol that points toward events pertaining to the psychological realm of the "second mind." As a universal, "archetypal" symbol the crucifix celebrates our individual capacity for "great expectations" and sacrifice. It celebrates our capacity to envision our "archetypal" dream that establishes the primacy of the responsible individual awakened to the psychological realm of the "second mind." It does not embrace the primacy of any institutional structure firmly entrenched, and seemingly content to live, at the social, economic level of the "first mind."

Therefore, according to the scientific, reasonable reading of our natural, experiential mythology, Christ emerges as the Western expression of the "archetypal" dreamer. Functioning in this role, he will appear in different "costumes" in Western literature—in American literature, for example—that seeks to awaken us to the reality of the "second mind" and thus to our individual sense of responsibility and sacrifice. The crucifix, finally, is not exclusively a Roman Catholic or Christian symbol. Rather, it is a universal symbol that enriches catholic literature of the "second mind." American literature provides only one reflection of that catholicity, but its "archetypal" vision could help govern the lives of individuals subject to its influence.

Ernest Hemingway, one of the acknowledged giants of American literature, felt that "all modern American literature comes from one book by Mark Twain called 'Huckleberry Finn.'" When we see Twain's work in the light of a reasonable interpretation of Christ, representing the Western "archetype" of the individual as dreamer, Hemingway's conclusion takes on greater significance. With Hemingway's thoughts in mind, if Huckleberry Finn isn't the quintessential American expression of Christ, and thus of the universal Hero "archetype," no such expression exists. If such were the case, any talk of the American Dream penetrating beyond the level of the historical realm of the "first mind" would be empty and hollow. But the opposite is true when we view Huckleberry Finn in the same reasonable manner we first apply to Christ in his role as the Western expression of the universal Hero "archetype." If we read Huck in this manner, focusing on the climactic incident where he tears up his note revealing Jim's whereabouts, Huck—like Christ—emerges as an incarnation of the dreamer who, having penetrated to the psychological realm of the "second mind," is crucified—alienated—in an institutionally structured world still wedded to the historical realm of the "first mind." As the embodiment of the American Dream from which "all modern American literature comes," if Huckleberry Finn is alienated, so is the dream itself. It can lie buried under the glitter of economic progress triumphantly symbolized by the proliferate Golden Arch.

If we want to live in fulfillment of the authentic American Dream, symbolized by Huckleberry Finn tearing up his informative note, and in further fulfillment of the "Archetypal Dream," symbolized by Christ enduring his crucifixion, we—as Americans—can begin by discovering our modern literary heritage. We can discover our modern mythological heritage built on the solid foundation of 'The Adventures of Huckleberry Finn' from which "all modern American literature comes." Taking a step further, we can discover that heritage as being a reflection of the Western literary heritage—the Western mythological heritage—solidly built on the bedrock foundation of the Garden of Eden story and the subsequent story of Christ. When we read them reasonably, these stories present events that occur in the psychological realm of the "second mind" rather than in the historical realm of the "first mind." Adam and Eve, Christ and Huckleberry Finn all have to disobey the more coercive authority of the "first mind" to obey its more evocative counterpart of the "second mind." In so doing they give concrete expression to the "adequate individual," the Heroic individual, who dares to dream of authentic, sacrificial love that cannot be limited to one occurrence in the realm of historical experience. Instead, it has to continue to occur throughout the realm of psychological experience if hope truly is to "spring eternal in the human breast."

Capitalism's Golden Arch hardly reflects hope of such magnitude and majesty, and neither does any equivalent economic symbol of "Caesar" that we may have rendered "unto God." However, a reasonable reading of the crucifix and its equivalent expressions, that belong to "God" and that we render "unto God" instead of neglecting them "unto nothing," unmistakably reflects that hope. The world of social, economic experience belongs to the realm of "Caesar" and the "first mind" while the world of mythological, psychological experience belongs to the realm of "God" and the "second mind." Dreams that we direct primarily toward "Caesar" and the "first mind" are not "archetypal" in nature—nor are their creators. On the other hand, dreams that we direct primarily toward "God" and the "second mind" fulfill that "archetypal" potential—as do their creators. Furthermore, responsible individuals—male or female without distinction or discrimination—can live such an "archetypal" dream. If we live for that dream, we live the "great expectations" and creative sacrifice that complete the beatific experience of the "second mind." That experience, finally, allows Jay Gatsby to "turn (ed) out all right in the end." The "foul dust that floated in the wake of his dreams," rather than Gatsby himself, "temporarily closed out" Nick Carraway's "interest in the abortive sorrows and short winded elations of men."

In the final analysis the American character, nor any individual character, regardless of ethnic or national "costume," holds no room for existential despair that can resign life solely to the level of economic promise expressed in symbols like the Golden Arch. Ultimately, the American Dream belongs to the level of the "second mind," the realm of the crucifix that is born out of authentic human experience with an authority, institutional or otherwise, not properly "human." In the Age of the Individual all of us share the responsibility to live the life of sacrifice, the "archetypal" life, eloquently expressed in the catholic symbol of the crucifix and, for Americans, just as eloquently reinforced by 'Huckleberry Finn' from which "all modern American literature comes." That literature, the backbone and soul of a great nation, does not celebrate dreamers of the "first mind." Such dreamers, although idealistic and noble, essentially are institutional people who assign their governing institution primacy over the individual. Thus dreamers identified with the "first mind" are not authentic incarnations of the Western or universal "archetype" of the "adequate individual"—the heroic individual, the dreamer, who believes in the primacy of the individual and who seeks to awaken all of us to the creative promise of the "second mind."

Idealistic dreams limited to the "first mind," unlike romantic dreams directed to the "second mind," ultimately are doomed and thus—no matter how inadvertently or unintentionally—end up contributing to a sense of rational despair. Trapped in such nihilism, individuals can turn to economic symbols such as the Golden Arch to "gather" their remaining energy "to a focus," relegating mythological symbols, such as the sun and the crucifix, to undeserved obscurity. The sun still is, and always will be, the giver of life, but now, overshadowed as it is by the glitter of the Golden Arch, it speaks only to the recreational interests of the "first mind"—if it speaks at all. And the crucifix—a symbol as natural as that of the sun, but devoid of any recreational use—speaks to neither the "first" nor the "second" mind. Seductively beckoning us to embrace its message of economic promise as the ultimate measure of human life, the Golden Arch speaks with "forked tongue." It is unable, therefore, to lift individual aspiration beyond the level reflected in the historical realm of the "first mind."

However, all is not lost. Standing at the crossroads without fear of the 21st century and beyond, we—as responsible individuals—can rediscover the sun and resurrect the crucifix. The sun continues to give life to the natural world that celebrates the individual human being as the center of our mythic imagination. And the crucifix, holding its creative promise of redemption geared to awakening the "second mind" that makes us properly "human," does not have to die. If we are worthy to survive and, even further, if we are worthy to "endure and prevail," we can acknowledge the duality of human nature, look beyond the immediate idealism of the "first mind" and discover, consciously, the ultimate romance of the "second mind." All of us then, as responsible individuals set free by accumulated experience and the discoveries of rational science, can prove ourselves worthy of identity with our natural, pagan ancestors for whom, however unconsciously, the mythological realm of the "second mind" revealed a world of mystery, wonder and infinite, romantic promise.

13

In Search of Morality

While we justifiably celebrate the impressive economic and technological triumphs of our Western world, we nonetheless live amidst a state of moral chaos and confusion. The recognizable crumbling of the moral order that has supported our Christian era isn't necessarily something we should welcome, considering the confusion and uncertainty that has accompanied the disintegration, but neither is it something we should fear. Most accurately, we should accept and affirm the disintegration of our traditional moral order as being the inevitable result of the continuing emergence of creative, individual inquiry and subsequent scientific discovery

Although the spirit of individual inquiry, identified with our ancient Greek predecessors, may be relatively new to our Christian era, it is nothing new to Western civilization. Evaluating the impact of science on myth, for example, Joseph Campbell tells us that by the year 275 BC the Greek thinker Aristarchus had calculated the fact that the earth revolves around the sun and not vice-versa as the Christian, institutional authority taught as late as the 17th century. Then, in accord with the same spirit of inquiry identified with Aristarchus, Galileo—looking through his telescope—discovered, with his own eyes, the conclusion his predecessor had reached 1800 years earlier. For his efforts, however, Galileo was condemned by the "Holy Office" of the "universal inquisition" for "having believed and held the doctrine which is false and contrary to the Holy and Divine Scripture that the sun is the center of the world, and that it does not move from east to west, and that the earth does move, and is not the center of the world." This reaction of the "Catholic and Apostolic Church of Rome," as Campbell recalls in 'Creative Mythology,' to Galileo's visible, experiential discovery demonstrates the pervasive institutional influence associated with the Church that, as Campbell tells us in his continuing analysis of science's impact on myth, exerted its authority "not for but against the search for disturbing truths."

Truths such as that which Galileo discovered are "disturbing" only if they threaten the status of the established moral testament the authority is supposed to uphold—convinced that their "Holy and Divine Scriptures" represent the source of The One, Revealed Truth. Any views that run contrary to that truth are then relegated to the level of heresy. However, with the appearance of Arthurian Romance, and specifically with the 13th century appearance of Wolfram von Eschenbach's 'Parzival' and Gottfried von Strassburg's 'Tristan,' we find evidence indicating that the power of the ecclesiastical authority and its imposed moral testament—supported by its "Holy and Divine Scriptures"—was beginning to crack. The Grail Hero, revealed in the work of Wolfram and Gottfried, finds himself honestly—and not rebelliously—at odds with the established social and moral order that imposed on the individual a morality built on the institution of marriage. That established order didn't seek to awaken anything resembling the Grail Hero's individual morality built on the concept of love. In fact, authority's imposed morality of marriage rested on the doctrine of original sin which supported and validated the Church's claims, as the earthly expression of Divine Authority, to primacy over the individual. But the appearance of the likes of 'Parzival' and 'Tristan,' identifying—if not celebrating—the individually oriented morality of love, reveals at least the beginning of a significant loss of faith in that institutional doctrine. The emergence of the Grail Hero, solidly built on the idea of individual self-worth more compatible with the substance of the Pelagian heresy, marks the beginning of the end of the dominance of institutional authority, standing firm on its imposed, original sin doctrine supported by its socially, politically and economically oriented moral testament.

The moral chaos and confusion that characterizes our contemporary world—and threatens to envelop the decades and centuries to come—testifies to the end of institutional dominance over the Western individual. If we can affirm the end of that dominance, we can embrace the vision of creative promise that accompanies the recognition of the inherent worth of the individual. To make such claims regarding individual dignity, free from the imposed constraints of original sin, would have been problematical in both the recent and remote past when the power and influence of institutional authority reigned supreme. But given the scientific triumphs and discoveries synonymous with our post-World War II era, to make such claims is both unproblematical and necessary if we are to discover a fresh sense of moral order to show us the way out of our current chaos. The doctrine of original sin, that supported the institutionally authorized morality of marriage, no longer is tenable in a scientific age whose discoveries disprove institutional clams to the peculiar historicity of the Christian Mythology.

The Christian authority's claim to supremacy, based on the historicity of its supporting mythology, no longer stands on seemingly firm ground. As evidenced by the resulting moral chaos and confusion that helps identify our contemporary social order, we have discovered en masse—and no matter how unwittingly—the truth to which inquiring, individual minds of the Middle Ages had the courage to reason.

In the wake of the turmoil that threatens to persist seemingly indefinitely, we easily can find ourselves without promise beyond that which our scientific technology has to offer. However, we can replace the institutionally imposed morality of marriage, solidly built on the premise of original sin, with a fresh moral testament—that of the individually evocative morality of love—totally free from those traditional restraints. If we remain ignorant of this inspired morality, we can look back towards the past, a retreat that is more reductive than creative, and continue to preserve the "shell (s) of a form (s) produced and left behind by lives once lived." The institutionally imposed morality of marriage is such a "form" that certainly has served its purpose. But just as certainly it did so at the expense of individual psychological maturation and the revelation of its accompanying morality of love—the Morality of Amor identified in the individual Grail Hero celebrated by Wolfram von Eschenbach and Gottfried von Strassburg, the medieval architects of a "Grand Design" supported, not refuted, by the wondrous discoveries of rational science.

Traditionally, authority taught the essentially sinful makeup of individuals and subsequently imposed its socially oriented morality of marriage, supported by the doctrine of original sin and its accompanying physical kingdoms of Heaven and Hell, on its subjects. Experience, on the other hand, traditionally reminded individuals of their capacity for love and subsequently sought to awaken its psychologically oriented morality supported by its doctrine of individual worth and its accompanying mythological kingdoms of Heaven and Hell. In obeying experience's morality of love, Wolfram's Parzival and Gottfried's Tristan "challenge Hell," but they direct their "challenge" to authority's—and not experience's—kingdom. By courageously challenging authority's "Hell," following in the footsteps of Adam and Eve in the similar Eden story, now read with curious eyes free from the visionary constraints of original sin, both Parzival and Tristan choose the bliss of experience's Heaven. In each case, referring to Adam and Eve, Parzival, Tristan or Christ as well, the Hero is alienated from his or her respective authority—Yahweh, the institutional Church or the Pharisees—that reserves places in its Heaven only for those individuals who obey its dictates. The established authority, regardless of its "costume," makes no allowances for any individually directed, and psychologically oriented, morality of love. As a result, the more socially oriented morality of marriage, which celebrates and preserves that primacy of the institution, reigns supreme.

When we "look long" at this conflict between experience and authority, expressed through stories like those of Adam and Eve, Parzival, Tristan and Christ, we can see that the claims of authority lack any basis in authentic, individual experience with mythology—inclusive of religion and literature—preserving the record of such experience. Furthermore, keeping that same conflict in mind, we can see that authority's claims lack any basis in rational, inquiring science as well. Creative scientific inquiry—from Aristarchus to Galileo and beyond—does not support any claims to the Christian Mythology being, primarily, a record of scientific and historical fact. Contemporary archeological and anthropological discoveries, dating the existence of human life thousands of years before Adam and Eve could have committed any original sin in any Garden of Eden, tell a different story. Among other things, those discoveries tell us that the morality of marriage, supported by traditional historic and scientific claims, has run its course—leaving us, as Western individuals, to search for a more appropriate moral testament or to live in perpetual chaos and confusion.

Unlike the mythological and historical Parzivals and Tristans of the Middle Ages, we do not have to "challenge Hell" if we decide to embark on our search. According to modern consciousness, enlightened by scientific discoveries, Hell no longer is a subterranean, physical Kingdom to which the architect of the original sin "Grand Design"—the celestial and separate God of Christian historicism—condemns disobedient souls. In fact, if we "look long" through the eyes of modern consciousness, those so-called disobedient souls may very well turn out to be obedient instead. The likes of Adam and Eve, Parzival, Tristan and Christ—expressions of the "Hero with a thousand faces"—are forced to disobey to obey. They have to disobey and "challenge" authority's "Hell" to obey experience and achieve the bliss of its Heaven. For Gottfried von Strassburg, as he states in his prologue to 'Tristan,' this Heaven is a psychological Kingdom of the here and now that "bears together in one heart its bitter sweetness and dear grief; its heart's delight and its pain of longing, dear life and sorrowful death, dear death and sorrowful life." And as Gottfried concludes: "in this world let me have my world, to be damned with it or to be saved."

The specter of Hell that plagued medieval obedient hearts open to the call of experience, the call of Amor that serves as the very source of our individuality and inherent worth, no longer plagues their contemporary counterparts. Thus none of us can blame fear of disobedience, and the subsequent banishment to the kingdom of eternal punishment, if we fail to embark on the quest for morality. We have to accept the blame if we ignore the quest to discover the morality of love, if we fail to respond to the challenge to heal the wound of the individual and collective "Waste Land" that characterizes our contemporary world inordinately identified with technological and economic promise. Admittedly, the morality of love, when compared to the socially recognizable morality of marriage, is an abstraction, but it's given concrete manifestation in the "Hero with a thousand faces." This Hero lives in our mythological world, waiting to be "made flesh" in the person of individual human beings, male and female without distinction or discrimination. The search for morality takes the individual beyond the boundaries of any institution to the discovery of the creative Self—the Hero—given first life in the inquiring minds of antiquity and then given second life in the worldly Grail Romance, in the "creative mythology" of Wolfram von Eschenbach and Gottfried von Strassburg.

Our contemporary chaotic era calls for nothing less than revolution. However, it does not call for the traditional action of social revolution to be carried out only in the economic, historical realm of individual existence. If nothing else, traditional, social revolutions are destructively archaic in an age that boasts such sophisticated technological weaponry. Furthermore, these revolutions, in the end, prove themselves to be—at best—expressions of Jung's "reforms by advances" which finally emerge as "deceptive sweetenings of existence" that "by no means increase the contentment and happiness of people on the whole." Such revolutions deceive because they don't encompass the "whole" individual in the first place. They ignore, and even disparage and condemn, the less visible—but nonetheless real—psychological, mythological realm of human existence. They ignore the realm to which any "creative mythology" speaks and the realm in which any authentic revolution properly should be fought.

The application of power in the name of duty, on any revolutionary battlefield and on any revolutionary scale, no longer is heroic. The battlefield focus has shifted to the psychological realm where it has belonged all along as indicated in the psychological, "creative mythology" of Wolfram and Gottfried. Both Parzival and Tristan are proficient in the ways of knightly warfare, but as heroes of "creative mythology" their primary conflict, that leads them to have to "challenge Hell," remains psychological in nature. As knights of their respective realms, they are compelled to uphold the social order firmly established on the foundation provided by the morality of marriage. But as individual human beings they are compelled to obey, contrary to the social order, the emerging morality of love—Dr. Eiseley's morality of "the responsible individual." Such individuals would not have to disobey in order to obey if the social order were based on this morality of love reflected in the knightly countenance of Parzival and Tristan—as well as in the crucified countenance of Christ. By ultimately choosing to obey the morality of experience—the morality of love—rather than the morality of authority—the morality of marriage—the Hero, in any one of a "thousand faces," proves to be an authentic revolutionary who seeks to correct, rather than to abolish, established, institutional authority.

When the revolutionary emphasis shifts to the psychological realm of human existence, the level of the "second mind," we discover the duty of the "responsible individual." Reflected in the Hero of that realm—the Hero of "creative mythology" from Adam and Eve to Christ to Parzival, Tristan and beyond—that duty directs one to live as an authentic revolutionary in proper obedience to the morality of experience, the morality of love. In the psychological realm of human existence every individual, male and female of every conceivable "face" without distinction or discrimination, can participate—as Hero—in the revolution. Only in that mythological realm can individual life hold any significant meaning. Only in the psychological realm of human existence can individual men and women live as Adams and Eves and Christs and Parzivals and Tristans. And only in that mythological, psychological realm—the level of the "second mind"—can individual men and women truly live with equality.

By awakening to the existence of this "second mind" and its morality of love, we allow ourselves to respond to the revolutionary call of the 21st century and the centuries to follow. We allow ourselves, finally, to respond to a call that lies at the very heart of the structuring mythology of the Christian West, unwittingly discovered—or perhaps rediscovered—in the 13th century by inquiring, responsible individuals such as Wolfram von Eschenbach and Gottfried von Strassburg. Looking through their honest eyes, Wolfram and Gottfried saw the "Waste Land" created by institutional imposition of a moral testament, the morality of marriage, that runs contrary to the moral testament, the morality of love, that identifies the "responsible individual." Experience alone—and not institutional imposition—awakens this healing testament in individual "listening hearts." Then, following in the footsteps of Wolfram and Gottfried, we can reawaken to the spirit of creative inquiry identified with the seemingly forgotten antiquity of our civilization.

Creative mythology speaks to the "second mind," the psychological realm of human existence. Its Adams and Eves, Christs, Parzivals and Tristans summon all of us to follow their lead and live our common destiny as Hero. In the psychological realm of human existence the individual is supposed to live as Hero to actively participate in the continuing process of creation that knows no beginning, as such, in time and therefore knows no end. As individuals, whose inherent worth is celebrated repeatedly in "creative mythology," we don't live in "purely durational time" that demands a physical and historical act of creation that, in turn, demands a commensurate physical and historical act of destruction. Rather, we live in "evolutionary time" that demands no such creative and destructive action. Instead, "evolutionary time" commands our participation in the continuing act of creation. And our contemporary time, within the continuing "evolution," commands recognition as "revolutionary time."

The psychological realm of the "second mind"—the mythological battlefield—rather than the social, economic realm of the "first mind"—the historical battlefield—provides us with the appropriate realm of revolution as defined by our contemporary era of moral chaos and confusion. As a result, the accompanying "revolutionary time" is a "creative time" as well. Such a "psychological revolution," as manifested in the "creative mythology" of Adam and Eve, Christ, Parzival and Tristan, represents a quiet and life-affirming maturational revolution that doesn't demand the violent dismantling of any unjust social structures. If the existing social structures are, in fact, unjust, we can't blame any injustices inherent in such structures themselves. We only can blame our own lack of psychological maturation and understanding. And when we "look long" at the Christian Mythology, free from the visionary constraints that accompany the doctrine of original sin, we discover the appropriate level of maturation manifested, repeatedly and consistently, in the "Hero with a thousand faces"—including those of Adam and Eve and Christ.

Thus the revolution demanded by our "revolutionary time" of life-defeating moral chaos and confusion represents nothing more than the fulfillment of our destiny as commanded by our mythological heritage whose "creativity" is revealed in the Medieval Romance of Wolfram von Eschenbach and Gottfried von Strassburg and finally reaffirmed by the discoveries of rational science. In turn, those discoveries free the individual, en masse, from the maturational constraints imposed by institutional demands of obedience to the doctrine of original sin. With our new found freedom we are allowed to discover the creative direction concretely expressed in our Christian Mythology. As individual initiators of this "psychological revolution," Wolfram and Gottfried were not rebellious malcontents seeking destruction of the existing social order. If anything, they were individual truth seekers following in the footsteps of their socially alienated, mythological predecessors—Adam and Eve and Christ—who sought to creatively correct that order "holding to the shells of forms produced and left behind by lives once lived."

If we persist in holding to such "forms," we will end up contributing more to our folly than to our fortune. Living amidst the undeniable discoveries of rational science, the individual human being—as revealed in "creative mythology" through "the Hero with a thousand faces"—has emerged as the true, creative force in our era of adventurous "revolutionary time." If we follow the creative, psychological path of heroic maturation, defined in "creative" Christian terms, we follow the Way of the Cross. This courageous journey, that takes us through the psychological realm of the "second mind," follows the path of Christ who then emerges as the New Testament, "archetypal" Hero of the Christian West in fulfillment of the Old Testament, mythological precedent established by Adam and Eve in the Garden of Eden. Having matured with the development of rational science, heroic individuals walk the creative path of the morality of love in quiet—but revolutionary—opposition to the institutionally authorized, but now archaic, path of the morality of marriage. In this "revolutionary time," marking the continuing evolution of the individual, the "responsible individual" represents the creative soul of any institutional structure. And the corresponding responsible institution will understand, as Jung reminds us, that "a million zeros" is still "zero."

For Loren Eiseley our era of moral chaos and confusion is "the whirlpool" that, he says, "can be conquered." To do so, as he reminds us in 'The Firmament of Time,' we "must learn to cultivate that which must never be permitted to enter the maelstrom—ourselves." A creative reading of our mythological heritage, that takes us into the relatively unexplored psychological realm of the "second mind," tells us that we can escape the "maelstrom" if we discover and live the mythologically oriented morality of love—following the lead of the Hero revealed in such "faces" as Adam and Eve, Christ, Parzival and Tristan. The stakes are high in our "revolutionary time" of conflict between the archaic morality of marriage and the still emerging, although oftentimes still totally ignored, morality of love. But the conflict that dominates our stormy "revolutionary time" was inevitable. Accepting that fact, we can discover the Hero only seemingly hidden behind a "thousand faces." We can "turn inward" as Dr. Eiseley suggests, for, as he continues, "if all knowledge is of the outside, if none is turned inward, if self-awareness fades into the blind acquiescence of the mass man, then the personal responsibility by which democracy lives will fade also."

To "turn inward" is not as abstract and nebulous as it may sound, and neither is it a turning away from responsibility. Individual works of "creative mythology," beginning with the foundation story of Adam and Eve in the Garden and continuing through Wolfram's 'Parzival,' Gottfried's 'Tristan' and beyond identify individual responsibility and illuminate our "inward" nature that reveals itself to be healthy and creative rather than pathological and destructive. And when we allow that "inward" nature to mature, even in the face of institutional opposition, we become "whole." Born out of an individual's experience with the "monstrous nature of life," and reinforcing the foundational Eden story, "creative mythology" gives expression to the human soul and celebrates the individual's capacity to live the morality of love. That morality of the "second mind"—rather than the morality of marriage as belonging to the "first mind"—represents the authentic creative power in our universe. In the world defined by the doctrine of original sin, the gods or God created human beings. But in the world now forever free from that influence, those same human beings clearly created the gods and God.

Accepting a world where we created the gods and God, and to further acknowledge the Serpent of Eden—the symbolic expression of the Divine Authority of the "second mind"—as the authentic God of "creative" Christianity, necessarily involves embracing the idea of a psychological revolution. But the time has come. At the very least, such an idea deserves our recognition as a creative thought that, when we take it seriously, seeks to illuminate the path of Dr. Eiseley's "personal responsibility." In a world now forever free from the imposed constraints inherent in the doctrine of original sin, that path is the path of redemption. Unfortunately, however, the redeemed individual—the heroic individual—living amidst the remnants of a social order built on the morality of marriage, continues to be crucified—alienated—by the very institutional structures that should lead the way and work for, rather than against, "the search for disturbing truths."

However, discovering the sense of "personal responsibility" that alone renders individual life meaningful does not involve discovering a "disturbing truth" in the first place. Instead, it involves discovering a "necessary truth" celebrated in the very mythological world—encompassing, in part, the worlds of Adam and Eve, Christ, Parzival and Tristan—that provides us with the foundation of our existence. If we continue to ignore that world or if we continue to associate it with lies, we work, no matter how unknowingly, more for the destruction of life than for its creation. In the final analysis, the wealth of experiential evidence, following thousands of years of human existence and preserved forever in the world of "creative mythology," profoundly supports Dr. Eiseley's creative conclusion that "the group may abstractly desire an ethic, theologians may preach an ethic, but no group ethic could, or should, replace the personal ethic of individual, responsible men." And the light that shines from "the Hero with a thousand faces" reveals that "personal ethic" to be the essence of the morality of love that then, provided we live in accord with its sacrificial demands, allows us to mature and embrace the highest level of moral behavior a human being can attain.

Admittedly, we find ourselves faced with a formidable task as we face our 21st century and the centuries to follow, but that same task is not impossible by any stretch of the imagination—at least not as long as the classroom exists. In Dr. Eiseley's words: "Schoolrooms are not and should not be the place where man learns only scientific techniques. They are the places where selfhood, what has been called 'the supreme instrument of knowledge,' is created." These "schoolrooms," being part of the "revolutionary process," can be manned by "revolutionary," heroic individuals—by Adams and Eves, Christs, Parzivals and Tristans—working within corrected, "revolutionary" and heroic institutions devoted to the awakening, rather than to the suppression, of the psychological realm of the "second mind." In this psychological realm of human existence all of us can fulfill our heroic destiny. We can live as incarnations of the morality of love. In the Age of the Individual that morality, initially manifested in the Serpent of Eden, assumes its place as God at a "revolutionary time" in our continuing evolution that has witnessed the death of God as traditionally defined by the archaic morality of marriage—one of the "shells of forms produced and left behind by lives once lived."

In finally assessing the task we face as we proceed with the 21st century of our Christian epoch, perhaps no one can exceed the level of eloquence Dr. Eiseley achieved in 'The Firmament of Time,' published in 1960 at the dawn of the age of manned celestial exploration:

> Let it be admitted that the world's problems are many and wearing, and the whirlpool runs fast. If we are to build a stable cultural structure above that which threatens to engulf us by changing our lives more rapidly than we can adjust our habits, it will only be by flinging over the torrent a structure as taught and flexible as a spider's web, a human society deeply self-conscious and undeceived by the waters that race beneath it, a society more literate, more appreciative of human worth than any society that has previously existed. That is the sole prescription, not for survival—which is meaningless—but for a society worthy to survive. It should be, in the end, a society more interested in the cultivation of noble minds than in change.

In short, Dr. Eiseley's vision describes a corrected society, one that is "worthy to survive," solidly built on the bedrock provided by the morality of love—the morality reflected in the "personal ethic of individual, responsible men" that heroically emerges out of the now ominous shadow of the "shells of forms left behind by lives once lived."

14

A Matter of Time

Fundamentally, as we've seen, life simply is a matter of time. Consequently, our understanding of time determines our understanding of life itself. For example, if we see time as having an historical beginning, we have to accept the fact that it has to have an historical ending as well. On the other hand, if we see time as just being time—there never was, and never will be, a time without time—we don't have to confront any historical ending. Then, life opens to endless possibilities, regardless of existing conditions. Psychologically speaking, we are better off seeing time as just being time, having no historical beginning and ending. With such realization and affirmation, we live free from any fear of the end of time or of the final end of life itself.

However, we can't simply declare that time has no historical beginning and ending. Without citing solid evidence to support that conclusion, we reduce the declaration to the level of mere talk, lacking the necessary conviction that can affect individual lives. For example, we are not convincing if we do nothing more than echo Alexander Pope's 18th century voice proclaiming that "hope springs eternal in the human breast." First of all, Pope's voice is not contemporary and secondly, despite his eloquence, he is not a scientist. Modern, rational individuals, products of Pope's Age of Reason, demand—and rightfully so—scientific proof to transform the language of mere talk into the language of firm conviction. When we "look long" with curious, honest eyes, we discover that the Western individual's quest to understand provides solid evidence that establishes the nature of time as just being time. As a result, life timelessly opens to infinite possibilities, granting Pope's vision the status of truth.

Now that we've entered the 21st century, we no longer can afford to pursue fruitless and irrational arguments over whether or not the nature of time is "durational" or "evolutionary." And we act even more fruitlessly and irrationally—as well as more destructively—if we live in resigned indifference to the subject. No less than the salvation of the Western individual is at stake, and the nature of time presents a topic that demands courageous confrontation, both collectively and individually. Whatever its implications, scientific research and inquiry into the antiquity of the earth has proven that time, indeed, is "evolutionary." Time is simply time, rendering any reasoning based on the opposite, "durational" premise archaic and, by now, even fearfully destructive.

Our Age of Rational Science has proven Alexander Pope's 18th century, poetic vision to be both insightful and scientifically accurate. The accumulated scientific evidence related to the nature of time and to the vastness of the universe itself renders our action destructively irrational if we hold on to the belief that time is "durational." In short, our own scientific discoveries demand that we grow into Pope's creative—and now rational—vision if we want to live with the dignity and decorum that accompanies a life free from fear. But in order to grow into Pope's rationally supported, romantic vision we have to question the very nature of our cherished Christian Revelation that, in contrast to the rational findings of scientific inquiry, defines time and creation as being "durational" rather than "evolutionary." Questioning that cherished revelation presents a formidable challenge, but our chaotic era demands that we humbly face—and accept—the responsibility.

At first glance the Christian Revelation and the discoveries of rational science, with regard to the nature of time, certainly contradict one another. The traditional, historical reading of the Christian Mythology tells of a definite, historical and supernatural act of creation that supports the belief in "durational" time as well as in what Dr. Eiseley identifies as the "catastrophic" explanation of the earth's various geological formations. As a result, that traditional reading assigns such work not to natural evolution but to the hand of the Creator. The discoveries of rational science, following the 18th century lead of geologist James Hutton, tell the story of a gradual act of natural evolution that supports the belief in "evolutionary" time as well as in an "evolutionary" explanation of the earth's geological formations. The work once assigned to the hand of a supernatural Creator now is assigned to the process of natural evolution. However, following a patient, second glance with regard to the nature of time, Christianity conflicts with the conclusions of rational, scientific inquiry only when it is offered as science. The subsequent reading renders Christianity irrational in the Age of Reason, leading us to conclude that it should be replaced by science. After all, scientific discoveries are infinitely more rational when we see them in relation to time and the topography of the earth which, in turn, proves to be far older than the 4,000 or so years authorized by the Bible.

A curious and patient second glance at the Christian Mythology, prompted by the demands of our age, reveals its ultimate compatibility with scientific discoveries where both revelations become life-supporting. Prior to the Age of Rational Science we could read our mythology as science without seriously threatening the necessary faith that results from authentic belief. But now that we are over 200 years into that age we cannot accept our Christian Revelation as scientific, historical truth without threatening that same faith which remains necessary as ever. We can only accept the discoveries of rational inquiry as science. And to lay to rest, forever, the first glance conflict between the claims of traditional Christian interpretation and the discoveries of rational science, we have to discover Christianity as being compatible with scientific inquiry and supportive of natural, "evolutionary" time.

When we rationally acknowledge "evolutionary," rather than "durational," time as the truth, we realize that the Christian Mythology comes from us, prompted by our recognition of time and the necessity of death that accompanies its continuing evolution. At first glance, once again, if we refer to Christianity as a creative revelation that comes from us, we appear to go so far as to deny creation and even the existence of God. However, upon patient second glance, such is not the case at all. If we see Christianity as being our own creative revelation, as our gift to ourselves, we redefine creation and God in light of the irrefutable discoveries of rational science. Creation does not have to be a physical, historical and supernatural act to be "real" and "true." And God does not have to be an historical, physical being living within that field to be "real" and "true," either. Within the field of natural, scientific "evolutionary" time creation becomes a continuing, psychological act in which all of us are supposed to participate. At the same time God becomes Jung's "psychic being" manifested repeatedly through the "Hero with a thousand faces." As one of those "faces," living in fulfillment of the Serpent of Eden, Christ then functions as the Hero of the "archetypal" Christian Revelation.

When we read it as a creative revelation that comes from ourselves, Christianity invites us to celebrate time rather than merely to consume it. In addition, because the discoveries of rational science reinforce the revelation, it commands a faith as irrefutable as those scientific conclusions. Moreover, when we acknowledge Christianity as being a revelation we created for ourselves, as part of our affirmation of the "evolutionary" nature of time, we see that it offers a faith continuing scientific inquiry only can strengthen. Therefore, when we accurately view it as a revelation we created, we cannot replace Christianity with science and its rational discoveries. On the contrary, it co-exists with scientific revelation and speaks to the psychological realm of our existence, or the level of the "second mind"—leaving the social, economic realm, the level of the "first mind," properly in the hands of science. Upon patient second glance, we learn that science needs mythology to give it soul and compassionate heart while mythology needs science to give it life now and in the decades and centuries to follow.

In order to see Christianity as our own creative revelation in affirmation of the "evolutionary" nature of time, reinforced—rather than refuted—by the discoveries of rational science, we have to rethink, and finally reject, the traditional institutional doctrine of original sin. Suggesting such action runs the risk of bordering on the blasphemous because it calls for us to rethink, and finally reject, the institutionally established, "durational" reading of the mythology that provides the foundation for Western life. But our "brave new world" of the 21st century and beyond, steeped in the discoveries of rational science, demands that we answer the call to participate in the continuing creation of life on our planet. The discoveries of rational science establish the authenticity of "evolutionary" time, indicating that the life-supporting structure built on the "durational" doctrine of original sin simply has run its "durational" course. If we fail to acknowledge that structure's obsolescence, we can contribute, no matter how unknowingly and inadvertently, to the destruction of life. If we retreat into the safety of that obsolescence, we can transform the structure itself into a lie.

When we see it through the lens of "evolutionary" time as having nothing to do with any historical original sin committed in any historical garden anywhere, we grant Christianity—as our own creative revelation—continuing life and allow it to function as a guiding force in our lives. The Garden of Eden story, according to its "evolutionary"—rather than its "durational"—reading, becomes more a story of the original avoidance of sin. In this scenario the Eden story celebrates the eating of the apple as being an action that is supposed to happen continuously as a necessary psychological event occurring in the boundless world of "evolutionary" time. When we read the story with fresh life, thanks to the liberating discoveries of rational science, we see the eating of the apple and the subsequent "fall" as being events we should seek to experience rather than avoid. The "fall" becomes a fall from ignorance that allows for the eventual emergence of natural wisdom—freely awakened by natural experience with the necessary monster that is life.

When we see the Fall of Man as a necessary fall from ignorance, the Serpent, who encourages Adam and Eve, emerges as the authentic God of Eden and of the Christian Mythology itself. That Serpent Power, then, symbolically expressed through the crucifix, is fully realized in Christ. The New Testament Christ, consequently, is not a "durational" creation trapped in historical time and irrelevant to any era falling outside a particular historical period. Rather, he is an "evolutionary" creation free from any historical boundaries and, therefore, psychologically alive for all time. As the Hero in one of a "thousand faces," he symbolically reveals the level of psychological maturation—identified as God in the "evolutionary" reading of the Christian Mythology—all individuals, male and female without distinction or discrimination, can attain. If we answer the natural call to "fall" from ignorance, we actively participate in the continuing, "evolutionary" act of creation that allows individuals to aspire to live, here and now, as incarnations of God..

Albert Camus—the noted French, "existential" philosopher, more "romantic" than "nihilistic,"—identified his 20th century as the "century of fear," and in his 1950 Nobel Prize Address, Faulkner reminded us that "the basest of all things is to be afraid." We can see that fear in the lack of dignity and decorum that marks the years following the conclusion of Vatican II, called—ostensibly—to bring the Catholic Church, and Christianity, into the nuclear era of the Age of Rational Science. As the results of that landmark ecumenical council reveal, the Church failed to see, no matter how inadvertently or unintentionally, Christianity's limitations when we read it primarily as a "durational" revelation given to us by our separate and superior God. Because it tells of life-supporting love that fallen individuals, corrupted by original sin in the Garden of Eden, cannot attain, that reading cannot inspire the romantic hope Alexander Pope proclaimed in the 18th century. Contrary to the teaching of Christianity's "evolutionary" reading, if Christ represents the only historical incarnation of the creative force of love which fallen individuals cannot attain, all hope is lost in a Sartrean, "absurd" world. And without the promise of love, save for the historical return of its Savior, this "absurd" world has to be meaningless as well.

If all hope is lost in an "absurd" world, then fear and despair reign supreme, helping to create a culture devoid of form and decorum. We can live in an economic frenzy—the "endless movement of pursuit" as Dr. Eiseley might say—as though we are dangerously close to running out of time. In such an environment claims of belief in the "durational" God, institutionally authorized in its "traditional" reading of the Christian Mythology, lack conviction. They can serve to mask the fear of time that eventually befalls the "durational" believer who, faced with contemporary scientific discoveries, finds it increasingly more difficult to continue to "wait for Godot." Psychological transformations certainly do not occur overnight, but they do occur once we creatively recognize the need and once we correctly identify the direction of the transformation.

In view of the discoveries of rational science, we cannot act destructively if we proclaim the death of God as traditionally defined by institutional authority. Nor can we act destructively if we proclaim the death of the belief in the authenticity of "durational" time. Even though that death results in the death of God as defined by any orthodox structure built on an archaic "durational" foundation, we act far more destructively if we ignore scientific discoveries or if we fearfully and ignorantly dismiss them as posing a threat to religious faith. The discoveries of rational science do not threaten that necessary faith. On the contrary, those discoveries—coinciding with the adventurous exploration of our earthly and celestial terrain—only serve to help uncover an indestructible faith built on the scientifically proven foundation of "evolutionary" time. Built on that scientifically, as well as naturally, solid foundation, this faith is firmly anchored in God. This God truly is Love, and individuals share the potential to live as incarnations of that word—The Word Made Flesh. Thus all of us, male and female without distinction or discrimination, have the potential to experience God while we live in this life here and now just as we experience it in "evolutionary" time.

When we read it in accord with the scientifically proven foundation of "evolutionary" time, the Christian Mythology proves itself to be an eloquent and timeless call to love that the serpent originally issued to Adam and Eve in their mythological Garden. When we "look long" within the boundless realm of "evolutionary" time, we recognize that Adam and Eve's refusal of the call would have guaranteed the eventual creation of life-defeating chaos far removed from life-supporting order. When we include him in that same boundless, "evolutionary" world, Christ emerges as a timeless expression of the Hero who answers the sacrificial call to love, the call of the serpent directed to individuals in this life here and now, only to find himself alienated from the social order that has failed to respond in kind.

Ideally, then, institutional authority should expand its orthodoxy to assume the role of an "evolutionary," Serpent authority—as opposed to continuing in that of a "durational," Yahwistic authority—to ease the pain of the crucified Savior and to encourage individuals to "follow Christ" on the archetypal path of "individuation"—the path of Amor identified and celebrated by the medieval troubadours. This sacrificial love, representing the highest level of moral behavior human beings can attain, has the power to unite us, as individuals, still divided—to a large extent—because of our failure to understand the nature of time.

If we, as individuals, cannot live as incarnations of Love, of Amor, our lives cannot hold any meaning beyond that offered by the social, economic level of our existence. And such a world, devoted primarily to the pursuit of economic promise, truly is a "Waste Land" populated by "hollow men" and "men of straw." But when we see it in relation to the scientifically proven foundation of "evolutionary" time, the Christian Mythology does not reveal the "evolutionary" Christ to be "hollow" and made of "straw."

However, as a 21st century individual, a "21st century child" as Joseph Campbell might say, I can't help thinking that we—in contrast to the nature of the revealed, "evolutionary" Christ—primarily live as such "men." And I can't help thinking that, in part, we owe our "hollowness," as manifested in our devotion to economic concerns, to our history of individual obedience to the dictates of an institutional authority whose limited vision—no matter how well the end may have justified the means—discouraged us from eating the apple and answering the sacrificial call of the serpent, the call of Amor. As a result, we were encouraged—in the name of obedience and love—to remain children and to avoid ultimate ascension to the very level of psychological maturation that renders us "wise as serpents" and "harmless as doves."

Even though I can't help lamenting "what man has made of man," I still can't help speculating on "what man could make of man." I can't help visualizing the psychological transformation of established, orthodox authority, and the subsequent transformation of individuals subject to its influence, from that of a "durational" authority built on a Yahwistic foundation to that of an "evolutionary" authority built on a Serpent foundation. I can't help thinking of 2,000 years of Yahwistic authority giving way to 2,000 years of Serpent authority, for example. And now that we're free from the visionary constraints associated with the doctrine of original sin, I can't help thinking of Christ being hailed as the fulfillment of the Serpent power. I can't help thinking of Christ being celebrated as a timeless expression of our capacity to respond to the natural call of love—the Amor command of the Serpent—and to live as incarnations of the experiential, and scientifically established, God of "evolutionary" time.

We in the Western world are experiencing a crisis of faith of colossal proportions. And I can't help seeing this crisis, manifested in the loss of cultural form and decorum that characterizes our day, as the inevitable result of living with the institutionally imposed, "durational" reading of the Christian Mythology. At the same time I can't help thinking if the Christian authority, and the individuals subject to its influence, remain unaware of the "evolutionary" reading of that revelation, we stand the chance of witnessing "the end of man" that Faulkner "declined to accept" in 1950. If we fail to acknowledge the loss of the traditional, "durational" reading of our cherished revelation and if we fail to search for a more substantial and indestructible reading of the Christian message, we may end up doomed to life in a "Waste Land" overrun with "hollow men" and "men of straw." We could strand ourselves in a moral and spiritual desert masked by exciting rhetoric pointing toward some promised future and further masked by inordinate devotion to economic concerns and the accompanying retail blight to which such devotion gives birth.

The Christian Mythology, when we read it in accord with the scientifically proven foundation of "evolutionary" time, celebrates "what man could make of man." Furthermore, the great "creative mythologies" of the West, both preceding and following the emergence of the Christian revelation, celebrate the same possibility. As American individuals, for instance, we can turn to 'The Adventures of Huckleberry Finn.' When we read it as part of, rather than apart from, the boundless world of "evolutionary" time, Mark Twain's foundational American classic proves itself to be a 19th century expression of the "archetypal" story of obedience we find in the tale of Eden and in the subsequent saga of Christ. Like the heroes who preceded him, Huckleberry Finn is a reflection of the "obedient heart" faced with what Dr. Jung would call a "conflict of duties." With reference to Jim, Miss Watson's runaway slave and his own companion in adventure, Huck has to decide if he should obey the established, social authority that demands he reveal Jim's secret whereabouts or his own emerging, natural authority—the inherent Serpent power or his "heart"—that commands him to answer the call to love. In effect, Huck has to disobey the imposed dictates of institutional authority if he is to obey the natural dictates of his "heart." He knows "it was a close place" and that he had "to decide forever betwixt two things." But in the end he tears up the note he had written revealing Jim's location, decides he'd rather go to authority's Hell for his disobedience, answers the call to love and points the way to psychological maturation. Huck answers the call of the Serpent initially heard in the Garden of Eden which we no longer can afford to misinterpret as being an historical garden experienced only by Adam and Eve.

Twain's "creative mythology" chronicles Huck Finn's "coming of age." Consciously or unconsciously, he built his story on the same "archetypal" foundation, one of having to disobey to obey, we can discover in the Garden of Eden story. And when we read that story in acceptance of "evolutionary" time, we free Adam and Eve from their entrapment, and contemporary irrelevance, in the "durational" world of historical time. When we free our mythological parents from their entrapment, we recognize the call of the Serpent, rather than the opposing call of Yahweh, as being the authentic call of creation. Reading Christianity's creation story in accord with the scientifically proven foundation of "evolutionary" time may not have been necessary in the seemingly simpler days of "durational" order, but those days are gone forever. A world of "evolutionary" order calls us to discover the "evolutionary" reading of our creation myth and of other, individual "creative mythologies" solidly built on its foundation. If we hope to make anything of ourselves worthy of respect and admiration in our scientifically supported "evolutionary" world, we are going to have to come of age in the manner we can identify in Adam and Eve, Christ and Huckleberry Finn. We are going to have to rediscover the God lost to us with the imposition of "durational" time. In the process we then can rediscover our capacity to live as incarnations of the Word that is God.

Huckleberry Finn can endure the alienation that follows his decision to obey the call of the Serpent because, knowingly or unknowingly, he discovered God. He discovered what Camus would refer to as "the invincible summer" that he discovered within himself "in the middle of winter" on "the road to Tipasa." Huck discovered the Grail which is the object of the romantic quest associated with the medieval Parzivals. He came of age not for a time but for all time and functions as a microcosmic expression of the coming of age of an entire American nation. To extend the metaphor even further, he functions as a microcosmic expression of the coming of age of an entire civilization faced with the prospects of decaying amidst the despair of "durational" time or of blossoming amidst the promise of "evolutionary" time.

I can't say that I'm optimistic about the prospects nor can I say that I'm pessimistic. But I think I can say that I'm romantic. In my romance I've found allies in the creators of the Garden of Eden story and the succeeding story of Christ as well as in Mark Twain as the creator of 'Huckleberry Finn.' In addition, I've found allies in Joseph Campbell with his exhaustive study of mythology—specifically "creative mythology"—in Loren Eiseley with his analysis of 'The Firmament of Time,' and in Carl Jung in his psychological works that essentially constitute, as he says, "the scientific rediscovery of ancient wisdom." Mr. Campbell and Dr. Jung together, along with Dr. Eiseley, specifically address the life-threatening spiritual and psychological crisis facing the contemporary individual. And I think Jung, in 'The Undiscovered Self,' most compassionately and most eloquently expresses the sentiments of the 21st century romantic:

> There is no sense in formulating the task that our age has forced upon us as a moral demand. We can, at best, merely make the psychological world situation so clear that it can be seen even by the myopic, and give utterance to words and ideas which even the hard of hearing can hear. We may hope for men of understanding and good will, and must therefore not grow weary of

reiterating those thoughts and insights which are needed. Finally, even the truth can spread and not only the popular lie.

By stripping the Hero of all his warrior and knightly glamour and by eliminating the impediment of "sivilized" language, Mark Twain, with 'The Adventures of Huckleberry Finn,' created a work that "can be seen even by the myopic," once we discover it as being of "evolutionary," salvatory value. The "psychological world situation," most specifically the Western world's, mirrors the psychological situation Huckleberry Finn faced and solved. Whether or not he realized as much, his solution allowed him to live as an incarnation of the Word that is God, was God and always will be God in our "evolutionary" world. Maybe "there is no sense in formulating the task that our age has forced upon us as a moral demand." But there is "sense" in calling for the discovery of the inspirational and healing power of the seemingly discredited, seemingly "durational" and scientifically irrelevant world of mythology which includes both religion and literature. That literature, reinforcing 'The Adventures of Huckleberry Finn' and built on the solid, "evolutionary" premise of obedience to the call of the Serpent, carries the religious power to affect and inspire "adequate individuals"—heroic individuals—to seek their destiny and live as expressions of the love, the Amor, that represents the creative power of the universe.

In the final analysis life truly is a matter of time. And in our "evolutionary" world, as opposed to any "durational" interpretation, hope does "spring eternal in the human breast." The "durational" reading of the Christian Mythology, built on the doctrine of original sin, is Jung's "program for life's morning" that by "the afternoon has become a lie." And none of us can "live the afternoon of life according to the program for life's morning." That "durational" program, built on the imposed premise of original sin, no longer can be presented, or accepted, as the truth in a world where scientific inquiry and discovery has proven time to be "evolutionary" instead. The "evolutionary" program for the continuing "afternoon of life," free from the visionary constraints of any inherited sin, calls for all of us to follow in the footsteps of Adam and Eve, Christ and Huckleberry Finn—all the time recognizing the fact that "even the truth can spread and not only the popular lie."

The End

About the Author

Emil Mihelich was born and raised in Butte, Montana, and has lived in Tacoma, Washington, for the past thirty-three years. He holds a BA Degree as well as an MA Degree in English, having earned both degrees from Gonzaga University in 1966 and 1973, respectively. He served as the Costello Teaching Fellow at Gonzaga from August of 1971 to May of 1973 and taught English in high school for eighteen years. A life-long sense of wonder about the world of mythology led him to recognize literature, and religion, as being part of that world. The subsequent journey of exploration—and discovery—ultimately gave birth to this book.

978-0-595-40214-4
0-595-40214-3

Printed in the United States
53961LVS00005B/115-129